MasterChef

COOKBOOK

MasterChef

C O O K B O O K

The Contestants and Judges of MasterChef
and JoAnn Cianciulli

RODALE

Notice

Mention of specific companies, organizations, or authorities in this book does not imply
endorsement by the author or publisher, nor does mention of specific companies,
organizations, or authorities imply that they endorse this book, its author, or the
publisher.

Internet addresses and telephone numbers given in this book were accurate
at the time it went to press.

Rodale books may be purchased for business or promotional use or for special sales.
For information, please write to: Special Markets Department, Rodale Inc.,
733 Third Avenue, New York, NY 10017.

Printed in the United States of America

Rodale Inc. makes every effort to use acid-free ⊗ recycled paper ♻.

Book design by Christina Gaugler

Food photographs by Vanessa Stump;
other photographs © 2010 by Reveille Independent LLC

Library of Congress Cataloging-in-Publication Data

Cianciulli, JoAnn.
    MasterChef cookbook / JoAnn Cianciulli.
            p.   cm.
    Includes index.
    ISBN-13 978–1–60529–123–9 pbk
    ISBN-10 1–60529–123–4 pbk
    1. Cookery.   I. Title.
TX714.C4966 2010
641.5—dc22   2010023235

Distributed to the trade by Macmillan

2 4 6 8 10 9 7 5 3 1   paperback

We inspire and enable people to improve their lives and the world around them.

Contents

Foreword by Joe Bastianich

After 20 years in the restaurant business, I've seen it all. From the young cook whose passion, dedication, and commitment transformed him into a world-class chef, to the waiter with an uncanny ability to make people happy who became my partner in three restaurants—the culinary world offers limitless opportunities. The restaurant and food business remains the last great bastion of meritocracy where hard work and talent are rewarded every day. In the early days of Becco (my first restaurant), it was my job to do it all—build the restaurant, buy the food, write the menu, serve the customers, and make the money. I evolved my ability and talent by *doing*. I was 23 years old at the time; the incredible opportunity of creating and launching a successful restaurant in the heart of Manhattan's Theater District prepared me for the successes and challenges I would face down the road.

The opportunity to become a judge on *MasterChef* has been the icing on a seven-layer-cake career. To be able to taste the food of the best amateur chefs in America is a rare opportunity and an honor. In a very real way, I have spent my entire professional life preparing for this unique challenge. Identifying and cultivating culinary talent is the essence of my job as a restaurateur. Since the day I hired my first line cook 20 years ago, I have been looking at the food on the plate to find the passion, talent, and soul of the person behind it. The objective of *MasterChef* is to find the best amateur chef in America, and I am clearly the guy for the job.

Tens of thousands of America's most talented, crazy, and ambitious home cooks auditioned for the show by serving us the plate that would distinguish them from the masses: their signature dish. Some dishes were simple, others were extremely complex. But each of them told us a lot about what America is cooking. From ethnic-inspired cuisine to regional favorites, down-home comfort food to four-star molecular cuisine, we saw and tasted it all. I can tell you firsthand that America's home cooks are making some pretty impressive food.

But just as impressive as the food we tasted were the cooks who created it. What struck me in a powerful way was the passion behind the food. These MasterChef hopefuls were not just accomplished home cooks; they were dreamers and doers looking to reach the culinary summit with the love, emotion, and the damn good food that they put on the plate.

Yet clearly, the search for America's first MasterChef was about much more than food. We were searching for that one individual who was able to speak to us through his or her culinary creations. Being a MasterChef is about having a passion for, and a deep commitment to, the unique art of cooking. The best chefs in the world can tell a story through the food they create, and the best amateur chefs in America are doing just that—telling us who they are, where they come from, and what inspires them through the simple act of cookery.

Becoming a judge on *MasterChef* was a welcome challenge for me. Having the opportunity to step out of the arena of professional cooks after so many years to see (and taste!) what America is really cooking gave me a new perspective on food. I've spent most of my career tasting and critiquing the creations of culinary school graduates and those under tutelage of the world's great chefs. *MasterChef* offered me the rare opportunity to taste the unaffected, untainted pure expressions of culinary passion that only the amateur cook can deliver. What an incredible opportunity.

During the *MasterChef* competition, the judges were able to taste some of the most exciting food that's being created in home kitchens across this great country. What struck me the most about the many plates we sampled was the diversity of the food presented to us. Each of these amateur cooks had a unique way of translating their passion and showing us on the plate, rather than telling us in person, why he or she deserved to be America's first-ever MasterChef.

For each contestant, the road was different. Some drew inspiration from their cultural heritage and recreated generations-old family recipes. Others celebrated the great bounty of American food by showcasing succulent Maine lobster, buttery Iowa beef, or pungent Oregon morel mushrooms. Still others were motivated by the show-stopping creations of the great American and European chefs. What all of them shared was the ability to create delicious food and a true love and devotion to the craft of cooking.

I can report to you that home cooking is alive and well in America. As a nation we are reuniting in the kitchen and around the dining room table to share our daily lives and our daily bread through the simple act of cooking. Processed and prepared foods are becoming a thing of the past as our home cooks celebrate what is local, sustainable, and real. This seemingly simple return to cooking fresh food and eating together is what will, in a real way, help us to overcome the seemingly insurmountable challenges posed by our modern lives. I can say with conviction that the great amateur cooks of America are playing a central role in healing our wounded society.

Watching the journey of our country's best home cooks on the *MasterChef* show, America will become intimately familiar with and ultimately invested in the quest to find the first-ever MasterChef. The journey is about more than the title; the triumphs and failures of each dish and its creator are a slice of our American story—the story of who we are, where we come from, and where we are going.

Foreword by Graham Elliot

These days, more attention than ever is being showered on celebrity—or, dare I say, rock star—chefs. And the cooking show genre is undergoing an explosive growth spurt. The real-life dramas that unfold on the small screen—coupled with amazing storytelling, competition, romance, and comedy—ensure that there's something we can all relate to, no matter who we are or where we come from. What sets *MasterChef* apart from the rest of the pack? I think its magic comes from the fact that its contestants are *not* trained profession-als or culinary school graduates. *MasterChef* contestants are real people, real Americans, cooking their hearts out for the chance to follow their dream.

MasterChef is already an international phenomenon, with hit shows in the UK and Australia that showcase each country's unique cooking style. Now it's America's turn to impress the world with our broad range of regional cuisines and to tell the story of our diverse ethnic fabric that makes us a true melting pot.

I'm still amazed that I was given the chance to teach, guide, and mentor the best home chefs in America. Working alongside Gordon Ramsay and Joe Bastianich was an honor. Gordon is without question the world's most famous TV chef and has almost as many Michelin stars under his belt as there are on the American flag. Joe is arguably the most successful restaurateur in the country, with more than 20 establishments coast to coast. Both have swagger and, most important, the skills to back them up.

But it was the amateur cooks we met who taught all of us an important lesson: You can't judge a book by its cover. We saw firsthand the hidden talent, passion, and drive that each and every contestant brought to the table—literally. These are people who understand that cooking isn't just about recipes or technique, but rather about finesse and touch and cooking with romance, sensuality, and, above all else, heart.

I am confident that this cookbook, much like the *MasterChef* show, will inspire you to cook for the people you love, reignite your cultural pride, and challenge you to think outside the recipe box.

Introduction
by Mark Koops, Executive Producer

Welcome to the *MasterChef Cookbook*! We hope that you get as much joy and fun out of this book as we have all had writing the book and producing the television show.

By way of back story, *MasterChef* first launched in the United Kingdom and has since grown into a world-wide phenomenon that offers everyday people the chance to live their dreams and express their passion for food and cooking. For some, the show is a once-in-a-lifetime opportunity to launch a career in the food industry; for others, it is a chance to showcase a treasured family recipe, learn new skills, or simply spend time doing what they love. Our goal in the *MasterChef Cookbook* is to provide you with similar inspiration and opportunity. We're here to teach you and treat you!

As with all new television shows, you never quite know what to expect when you begin the journey. When we started our search for the nation's first MasterChef, we set up casting calls around the country. The first city on our tour also happened to be one of the culinary capitals of the world: New York City. We were blown away to see a line that wrapped around the block, filled with people from all walks of life, cultures, and ages. Not only were we impressed by the size and diversity of the crowd, we were also wowed by the incredibly positive, warm attitude people had. No one was complaining, no one was being rude (and remember, this was New York!), and no one was trying to jump the line. Everyone was simply having a great time, swapping recipes, passing on tips, and giving advice.

We could fill another book with the stories of the people we met on that casting call, but for now, here's a glimpse of some of the incredible people we encountered: a harp player who slept in her car on the streets of New York to be first in line; a doctor who was inspired to cook by the family cookbook her deceased mother bequeathed to her; a precocious 12-year-old who knew more about cooking than any of us; and an inspiring young man born with only three fingers on each hand who didn't let his disability stop him from tackling anything—including our judges!

Ten cities and thousands of miles (and online applications) later, we retreated to our offices, faced with the impossible task of whittling down the list of thousands of hopefuls to just 50 people whom we would invite to Los Angeles to prepare their signature dish for our judges (more on them later). As we were making our choices, our production crew was feverishly constructing the *MasterChef* studio in downtown Los Angeles. In a matter of days, an old empty warehouse was transformed into a state-of-the-art cooking theater that would soon host our aspiring contestants.

The first few days proved to be a nerve-racking whirlwind for the production crew and our hopefuls alike. The first challenge was simple: Create one signature dish in one hour. If it impresses the judges, you win an apron and move on to the next round of competition. However, this task proved neither simple nor straightforward, and only 30 contestants would be able to move on. Our judges tasted every conceivable type of food, and you will find the recipes for many of these memorable dishes throughout the pages of this book. We can guarantee that Jenna's Stuffed Buttermilk Pancakes (page 26) will soon become a family favorite, while Jake's Eclectic Surf and Turf (page 175) is perfect for any dinner party.

The 30 remaining contestants barely had a chance to catch their breath before facing two challenges that would test their technique and creativity. One of our favorite memories is seeing the contestants' faces as they walked into a cavernous warehouse and discovered that they had to chop and dice pounds and pounds of onions to demonstrate their knife skills (see page 30 to learn how to master this skill yourself!). Not all the tears that ensued were caused by the onions, but they were all real, as six more contestants saw their dreams end when Graham Elliot and Gordon Ramsay asked them to put down their knives and take off their aprons.

Twenty-four were now one step away from making it into the MasterChef kitchen. But to earn that spot, they had to impress our judges with their culinary creativity by making a dish with one egg and the ingredients available in our pantry (see page 13 for tips on stocking your own pantry). If you watched this episode, you know just how much can be done with a single egg! The contestants served up mouthwatering meals for all occasions, and now so can you—from Tony's Egg in Purgatory (page 28) to Tracy's Banana Pudding Napoleon (page 212). The judges somehow stayed focused, and a long day came to an end when Avis's delicious Old-School Deviled Egg (page 60) won her the 14th and final spot in the next round.

Over the next few weeks, our final 14 withstood every type of challenge imaginable that stretched their creativity, challenged their technique, tested their taste buds, and drove them to new heights. The Mystery Boxes surprised them with an assortment of ingredients—perhaps none more so than the live crabs (check out Lee's delicious answer to the challenge, Dungeness Crab Salad with Fresh Avocado and Gazpacho Andalouse Sauce, on page 70). The Invention Tests, to quote Gordon, put "three stunning ingredients" in front of the Mystery Box challenge winner and gave him or her the power to choose the main ingredient for that challenge. The Field Challenges forced the contestants to leave the comfort of the kitchen and literally do everything from feed an army (or in this case Marines) to cater a picture-perfect wedding. And last, but by no means least, the Pressure Tests were exactly that: high-stakes, high-drama, pressure-filled challenges where one wrong ingredient could send you home. The contestants continually surprised and confounded our judges with their efforts, and to watch each and every one of them grow in confidence and stature over the course of the competition was inspiring to us all.

Throughout this book, you'll find easy-to-follow instructions that will help you master all of the culinary basics as well as a wide variety of delicious recipes for every occasion, from appetizers to desserts. And Joe Bastianich's simple wine-pairing suggestions (see page 18) will ensure that your meals have the perfect finishing touch. Most important, we hope that with every page you read and every recipe you make, you fall in love with food all over again. Even if you aren't familiar with some of the ingredients or think you're not experienced enough to tackle the more complex dishes, we urge you to try, experiment, and expand your culinary horizons. Only by trying will you learn and grow as a chef.

Finally, we'd like to say a huge thank-you to our incredible judges: Gordon Ramsay, Joe Bastianich, and Graham Elliot, who are passionate and articulate about all things culinary and so much more. Their input and knowledge elevate this book, as they did the show, and we hope you have as much fun learning from them as we did. If you imagine them watching over you as you cook these recipes, we guarantee it will bring out your A-game and help you produce great food.

So we're off to make Dave's New England Clam Chowder (page 79), Whitney's Southern-Fried Pork Chop (page 169), and Sheetal's Flaky Apple Pie (page 234). What's for dinner at your house?

Keep watching, keep cooking, and have fun!

Gearing Up

Building a cook's kitchen is an exciting challenge. It's normal to feel a little over-whelmed in kitchenware shops, surrounded by all of those gleaming copper pots and pans, sharp knives, and high-tech gadgets. Don't be intimidated! You just need to know the basics: the essential tools you'll need to prepare even the most intricate recipe. Steer clear of cutesy, colorful gadgets and cheap knives that never need to be sharpened. Spend your money wisely to get the most out of your culinary budget.

When it comes to kitchen equipment, the expression "You get what you pay for" could not be truer. A few good pieces will last a lifetime (and sometimes longer). Most well-made kitchen equipment comes with a lifetime replacement warranty. In the long run, it's more economical to buy a piece that's backed by a good guaran-tee than one you'll have to replace over and over. The following guidelines will help you gather the equipment that no MasterChef should be without.

MasterChef Equipment Basics

KNIVES

These are the tools you'll use most often in the kitchen, and a great chef's knife is symbolic of a serious cook. A high-quality knife is worth the investment and will last for years if you treat it properly and have it professionally sharpened once in a while. Look for knives that will last, with a high-carbon stainless steel blade that stays sharp and doesn't rust. The handles may be wooden or plastic; the important thing to look for is a blade that extends to the end of the handle, which is called *full tang*. Shop around and see what brand fits your hand well and feels comfortable and balanced when you hold it.

These three kitchen knives can be used to cover a multitude of kitchen tasks:

Chef's knife, 8-inch blade: Everyone needs a proper chef's knife—it is the most important tool in the kitchen. This is an all-purpose knife, used for a wide variety of cutting tasks, from slicing onions to chopping herbs to carving meat.

Paring knife: This is the second most used knife in the kitchen. With a 3- to 4-inch blade, the small knife is designed for precise tasks such as peeling and trimming.

Serrated knife: Serrated knives are good not only for cutting bread but also for slicing fragile fruits and soft vegetables, such as tomatoes. The teeth on serrated knives can't be sharpened, so once they are dull, the knife should be replaced.

Cutlery Care

A magnetic knife strip that mounts to your kitchen wall is the safest and best way to store your knives. Piling sharp knives in a drawer is dangerous and can nick the blades. Wooden knife blocks trap moisture and are difficult to clean; the moisture that gets trapped in those narrow slits can be a breeding ground for bacteria. Plus the blocks take up precious counter space! Never put knives in the dishwasher. A quick rinse with hot water and a soapy sponge is all you need to keep them clean. Be sure to dry them well.

The proper way to maintain the edge of the blade is using a whetstone. If you do not have a whetstone and are not inclined to learn how to use one, have your knives professionally sharpened at a local cutlery or hardware store. A sharp knife not only cuts better but is safer. A dull knife forces you to use more pressure to cut the food, causing your hand to slip. Depending on how much you cook, it's a good idea to sharpen your knives every few months.

Use a sharpening steel to maintain the edges in between sharpenings. A steel does not sharpen knives, but it does keep the edges straight and aligned. A few even strokes on both sides of the blade right before you start chopping will keep those potato slices paper-thin.

Respect your knives: Start with good ones, keep them sharp, and they will be your friends.

CUTTING BOARDS

Cutting boards come in a variety of materials—such as wood, plastic, marble, or glass—and in different shapes, such as rectangular, square, or round. Marble and glass boards aren't particularly good for your knives as their surface is too hard and dulls the blade. Plastic cutting boards are dishwasher safe and very easy to clean. You'll always need more than one cutting board. Keep a designated plastic cutting board for poultry to prevent cross-contamination. It's also a good idea to keep a small board used only for chopping garlic to avoid transferring its strong odor to other ingredients.

Wooden cutting boards are heavy, and some of the more decorative boards are quite attractive for displaying in your kitchen. These boards give a truly resistant cutting surface while being kind to the blade's sharp edge. Always be scrupulous about scrubbing boards after use in hot soapy water, and dry them well. Never submerge wooden boards in a sink of water. Wood is porous and will soak up water, causing the cutting board to warp and crack when it dries.

Rub mineral oil on wooden cutting boards to prevent staining and absorption of food odors and bacteria. The oil prevents knife marks on the board and keeps the wood looking new. Never use cooking oils to treat a cutting board—in time, the wood will reek of rancid oil. An occasional sanding will return a wooden board to a smooth luster, if needed.

Sanitize both wood and plastic cutting boards with a diluted chlorine bleach or vinegar solution consisting of 1 tablespoon of bleach or white vinegar in 1 cup of water.

To keep your cutting board from sliding around on the counter, put a couple of damp paper towels underneath it.

COOKWARE

A few good-quality pots and pans in varying sizes are an excellent start when outfitting a kitchen. Fancy copper cookware is by no means a necessity to be a great cook. There are a lot of choices out there. Seek out reputable brands, and feel for weight. Here are some essential pieces that will help you cook with confidence:

Medium-size saucepans, 2-quart and 3-quart capacity: These are good for everything from making sauces to boiling an egg and cooking rice.

Large stockpot: You'll use this for cooking pasta, soups, and stews.

Dutch oven (or covered casserole), 4- or 5-quart capacity: This stove-to-oven-to-table vessel is an essential piece of cookware, perfect for braises and simmering dishes such as chili.

Skillets, 10 inches and 12 inches in diameter: Skillets are your everyday sauté pans—you'll use them regularly.

A well-seasoned cast-iron skillet, preferably an heirloom: These are great for baking cornbread and cooking other rich foods. Cast-iron skillets should never be scrubbed—the idea is to "season" a skillet. Gently clean after each use.

Nonstick omelet pan, 8 inches in diameter: This will help you create perfect eggs in the morning.

Buy other pots and pans as you need them. For instance, if you find that you're doing a lot of grilling, it might be worth it to invest in a ridged grill pan. If you cook a lot of Asian dishes, it would probably make sense to buy a wok. If you plan on hosting Thanksgiving each year at your house, invest in a durable roasting pan to make memorable turkeys.

Cookware should be ovenproof (no plastic handles!) so it can transfer from the stove top to the oven. It is both useful and practical to pan-roast a chicken breast by searing it first, then finishing it in the oven. Look

for well-made, heavy pots and pans. Heavier pans distribute heat evenly and prevent hot spots so food doesn't burn.

BAKEWARE

Pick up several baking pans in different sizes. They can be used to bake desserts as well as cook savory ingredients, such as root vegetables, fish, and meat. They have a small lip around the sides, so heat circulates evenly around the food. A 9 × 13-inch glass or ceramic baking dish is perfect for roasting a chicken, baking brownies, and making macaroni and cheese.

If you enjoy baking and make a lot of desserts, you should purchase a 9-inch pie plate and two 9-inch cake pans. It's also helpful to have a standard 12-cup muffin pan.

In the MasterChef Kitchen

Here's a list of the basic equipment that the contestants used most often in the *MasterChef* kitchen. It's a good idea to stock your kitchen with these tools as well.

Mixing bowls: Keep a variety of sizes in both glass and stainless steel. Plastic bowls are hard to clean properly and are not good for whipping cream or egg whites.

***Mise en place* bowls:** Use small- to medium-size bowls and ramekins for storing chopped ingredients or measured portions of liquids or solids as you prep for a meal.

Measuring cups: You'll need a set for liquid ingredients and a set for dry ingredients. It's best to use cups made of glass, plastic, or stainless steel.

Measuring spoons: A set of measuring spoons is essential for baking, where precision is crucial.

Scales: The most accurate way to measure dry ingredients is to weigh them.

Thermometers: An instant-read thermometer inserted into cooked meat is the most accurate way to determine proper doneness. Candy or deep-fry thermometers are designed to read the temperature of hot sugar or oil and are not reliable when used for meat.

Colander: Use a metal or plastic colander to strain pasta and blanched vegetables.

Fine-mesh sieve: Use this for straining sauces and dusting dessert dishes with confectioners' sugar or cocoa powder.

OTHER TOOLS

Mandoline: This tool slices vegetables very thinly and uniformly. Be sure to use the guard.

Graters: A box grater with coarse and fine holes and a handheld microplane are excellent for grating citrus zest, nutmeg, chocolate, and cheese.

Vegetable peelers: These quickly and easily remove vegetable and fruit skins and can also be used to shave cheese.

Pastry brushes: Use a brush to spread and evenly distribute melted butter, marinades, or an egg wash.

Whisks: Helpful for aerating food, such as egg whites, and beating sauces to create an emulsion.

Flat spatulas: Great for lifting and turning food, such as pancakes. A thin, flexible "fish" spatula is a chef favorite—it works with precision on anything tricky to turn, from Dover sole to crepes to eggs.

Rubber spatulas: Made from heatproof silicone, these are used for folding together batters, scraping bowls clean, and stirring delicate sauces.

Icing spatulas: The long, narrow spatula may be straight or offset and is used in baking for spreading fillings and icing.

Wooden spoons: Useful for stirring sauces.

Ladles: Needed to transfer sauces or soups to serving dishes without a lot of mess.

Slotted spoons/skimmers: Made of perforated metal or mesh, these are useful for removing foods from hot liquids or skimming foam from simmering stock.

Tongs: Handy for turning food in a pan or on the grill as well as for lifting food from hot liquid.

Ring molds or biscuit cutters: These cookie cutter–like molds come in various shapes and sizes and are terrific for cutting pastry or creating a refined plate presentation.

Kitchen string: Use for trussing or tying meat.

Silpat: If you do a lot of baking, these thin mats are lifesavers for keeping fragile foods from sticking to a cookie sheet or baking pan.

Salad spinner: Washing greens and drying them well with a spinner will keep them fresher longer.

Wine opener: A good-quality wine opener will make life a lot easier.

Can opener: It doesn't have to be fancy; it just has to be sharp, clean, and easy to use.

Peppermill: Keep this near the stove for handy seasoning with freshly ground pepper.

SMALL APPLIANCES

Food processor: Invaluable for chopping, slicing, shredding, making dough, and puréeing vegetables, soups, and sauces.

Blender: Great for blending drinks and aerating sauces.

Handheld immersion blender: This allows you to purée soups and sauces right in the pan, which saves you the extra step of transferring hot mixtures to a blender or food processor and back.

Electric mixers: If you bake frequently, you will want both a powerful standing mixer and a small handheld mixer. The standing mixer works best for dough and batter. The handheld whips up egg whites, butter, and heavy cream.

Mortar and pestle or coffee grinder: Useful for grinding small amounts of spices or making pastes.

Stocking Up

A true hallmark of a MasterChef is a perfectly stocked pantry. After all, a finished dish is only as good as the ingredients used to make it. From the oil in the pan to the herbs used as a garnish, every ingredient can help or hurt the overall flavor of a dish. The ability to improvise and create a fabulous meal from simple ingredients is an enviable skill and the true test of a resourceful cook. A well-stocked pantry allows you to cook with confidence and think on your feet.

In addition to stocking basic staples such as salt, sugar, butter, and canned tomatoes, look for new flavors to add to your pantry, such as canned chipotle chiles, rice vinegar, and tahini paste. Cooking with unusual ingredients from around the world will open up your cooking repertoire.

Use the following list as a guideline for stocking your shelves at home. You don't need to run out and purchase all of these items at once. None of us shop, cook, or eat in exactly the same way. The goal is to keep your pantry full of the items that you use most often.

The MasterChef Pantry

DRY INGREDIENTS

Flour: all-purpose, cake, and semolina

Sugar: granulated, brown, confectioners', and honey

Bread crumbs: plain and panko (Japanese)

Corn: cornmeal, cornstarch, and polenta

Leavening: baking powder, baking soda, and active dry yeast

Rice: jasmine, brown, and arborio

Grains: couscous, Israeli couscous, farro, bulgur, and quinoa

Dried pasta and noodles: spaghetti, penne, soba noodles, and rice noodles

Dried beans and legumes: lentils, white beans, black beans, and chickpeas

Chocolate: cocoa powder and baking squares of various cacao percentages

Dried fruit: apricots, figs, dates, raisins, golden raisins, and cranberries

Dried porcini mushrooms

Coconut flakes

Vanilla beans

Coffee

BOTTLES, JARS, AND CANS

Oil: extra-virgin olive oil, vegetable, peanut, sesame, and cooking spray

Vinegar: white, balsamic, red, sherry, and rice

Wine: white, red, mirin, Marsala, port, and brandy

Capers

Black and green olives

Tahini paste

Wasabi paste

Miso paste

Peanut butter

Worcestershire sauce

Soy sauce

Fish sauce (*nam pla*)

Vanilla extract

Dijon mustard

Ketchup

Hot sauce: Tabasco, Sriracha, and sambal

Beans: white, garbanzo, black, and pinto

Tomatoes: whole, diced, crushed, paste, and sundried

Chipotle chiles in adobo sauce

Tuna and anchovies in oil

FRIDGE AND FREEZER

Garlic, onions, and shallots

Bacon

Unsalted butter

Whole milk

Heavy cream

Crème fraîche

Sour cream

Plain yogurt

Cheese: Parmesan, cream cheese, goat, Cheddar, blue, ricotta

Eggs

Wonton wrappers

Phyllo dough

Puff pastry

Nuts and seeds (these are best kept in the freezer)

Herbs: basil, oregano, rosemary, thyme (fresh herbs are best kept in the refrigerator)

A note on using fresh herbs

Most chefs agree: There is no comparison, flavor-wise, between fresh herbs and dried (with the exception of dried oregano). Fresh herbs are widely available and add intense, bright flavor to foods.

Winter herbs such as rosemary, sage, thyme, and bay leaves lend themselves to heartier foods (such as Veal Saltimbocca, page 201, or Herb and Panko-Crusted Rack of Lamb, page 207). These herbs add an earthy depth and hold up to braising and a long, slow-cooking process. Cooking releases their natural oils and mellows their intense flavor. Summer herbs, on the other hand, add a sunny flavor punch and are generally better if chopped and tossed in the dish at the last minute. Some staples are basil, cilantro, and mint. Flat-leaf parsley complements just about anything.

Always keep a variety of herbs in the crisper. Try to buy them freshly cut, by the bunch.

SPICE RACK

Variety, we all know, is the spice of life, but it's also true that spices add incredible variety to your culinary endeavors. When it comes to seasoning with spices, follow your nose. You'll quickly develop a sense of how these flavorings complement each dish.

Dried spices are a flavor vehicle for taking the dish anywhere you want it to go. Certain spice combinations are indigenous to specific cultures and cuisines. For example, clove, coriander, and fennel seed are often used in Middle Eastern cooking. Cumin, paprika, and cinnamon will bring you the flavors of Latin-American cuisine.

Below you'll find a list of the spices any MasterChef should keep on hand. Store your spices in airtight containers away from sunlight and oven heat. If you're unsure of a spice's freshness, take a sniff—if it's odorless or smells stale, toss it and restock.

Allspice, ground

Bay leaf

Black peppercorns

Cayenne pepper

Chinese five-spice powder

Cinnamon, ground and whole sticks

Cloves, whole

Coriander seed

Cream of tartar

Cumin, ground and whole

Fennel seed

Kosher salt

Mustard, dried

Nutmeg, whole

Oregano

Smoked paprika

Red-pepper flakes

Saffron threads

A note on salt and pepper

Salt, along with its partner, pepper, are two of the most familiar and important seasonings in any cook's kitchen. A good steak cooked without seasoning is just a piece of meat. Salt enhances and intensifies the flavor of foods, even in sweets such as candy, cookies, and cakes. A light seasoning of salt smooths out any bitterness and enhances the natural flavor of food. Salt also intensifies aromas, making them more apparent and seductive. Pepper brings food alive with a subtly spicy kick and balances the flavor of the salt.

For everyday use, kosher salt is the chef's choice for cooking. The additive-free, coarse-grained salt is far superior to iodized table salt, which imparts an unpleasant metallic, medicinal flavor to food. These days, a wide range of gourmet salts and peppercorns are available in every color in the rainbow and are being used to add complexity and nuance to all kinds of dishes. Add a few to your pantry and try them out.

Remember to taste food constantly throughout the cooking process. Seasoning is not about measuring; it's about tasting as you go and layering salt and pepper in stages to build flavor. Whether you are preparing a simple salad or a complex and lengthy braise, season when you begin—then cook, taste, cook some more, taste again, season, and just before serving, taste again and adjust the seasoning. As long as you season in judicious amounts, you shouldn't ever have to worry about overseasoning.

Wine Notes
by Joe Bastianich

The story of the American dinner table doesn't begin and end with the recipe. Over the last several decades, we've also come to embrace wine as an essential companion to our meals. Wine complements our food and our lives, adding elements of flavor, virtue, and happiness.

As we learn more about the food we eat and where it comes from, we are gaining acceptance of wine as an agricultural product that expresses its own *terroir*, or place of origin. Wine consumption is increasing more rapidly than any other (alcoholic) beverage in our country as quality is on the rise, pricing has become more competitive, and information and education are more widely available. The foodie culture that permeates our society is being washed down with a great big glass of wine.

Wine making may appear to be a simple undertaking. Grapes are grown, then crushed, juice is fermented, pressed, and voilà . . . you have wine. It really is and should be that easy, but the very essence of wine is in the details. Every winemaker imparts his or her individual character into each bottle. Good wine cannot be mass-produced.

There are many variations on the technique of making and storing wine that affect its taste. Toasted oak barrels can add richness and complexity; extended contact with skins and seed can add structure and tannin; controlling fermentation temperatures can coax out minerality and delicate aromas. These along with a myriad of other choices allow a winemaker to personalize his or her creation.

To fully experience and appreciate any wine, you must engage all of your senses. First and most often overlooked, it is important to consider the color of a wine. Hold it up to a light source, against white background. What colors do you see? Is your white wine golden? Does it have a glistening green edge? These visual observations can give you insight into what the wine will smell and taste like. Red wines may reveal even more subtlties. Hold your glass of red up to the light. Is the tone brick in the center, fading to burnt orange on the ring? Is it a light red rose that reflects light or a dense purple, syrupy and thick? Carefully observing the wine in your glass will help you to evaluate it.

The "nose" of a wine reveals even more about how it will taste. After observing your wine in the light, swirl your glass (to get air into the wine) and take a deep sniff—put your nose right inside the glass and inhale the aroma. Smelling the wine will release a cascade of sensations directly to your brain. Even once you finally taste it by pouring it onto your palate (in your mouth), you are still effectively smelling as the wine enters your body filling all your air passages with its scent. The tasting is complete after you swallow the wine and experience the composition of the wine—its tannins, acidity, and alcohol.

Although understanding the technical components of wine tasting is important, the most important aspect of tasting is being able to identify the wines you like and why you like them. The best way (perhaps the only way) to do this is to taste lots of different wines and record your experiences. Take tasting notes if it helps you. The objective is to create a database of wine experiences that you can refer to when seeking out a specific wine or trying to evaluate a new one.

We choose the wines we drink based on lots of different criteria. Sometimes we simply crave the specific flavor profile of a wine we know and love. Other times we want to sip something that suits our mood or the season, or that reminds us of a particular time or place. Most often, we choose a wine to complement the food we plan to eat. As cooks, we spend so much time, care, and effort selecting and preparing our ingredients, that choosing complementary wines should also be a necessary part of creating the best possible dining experience. In fact, pairing food and wine has become the central theme to our dinner parties and entertaining style.

The recipes contained in this book represent the very best of what America is cooking at home. The flavors are bold; the styles unique. As diverse and personal as these recipes are, there is a perfect wine to pair with each of them. The beauty of pairing wine and food is that it is up to your very own personal taste. The one thing that every food and wine pairing has in common is that it causes us to stop and think about the sensory input we receive from food and wine consumed together.

The suggestions I offer on the following pages are a simple overview of some of my favorite pairings. But the ultimate magic of food and wine shared at the table is created by every aspiring MasterChef who puts his or her passion on the plate and pours out a bottle among friends.

BREAKFAST

Prosecco: The perfect brunch drink; it pairs nicely with virtually anything. You could even make Bellinis to impress your guests. Try using fruit purees such as peach, green apple, or pomegranate.

Moscato: This fruity Italian wine is delicious with sweet breakfast dishes such as Cinnamon-Orange French Toast (page 40).

SOUPS, SALADS & STARTERS

Albarino, chenin blanc, and Arnaiz: These flinty, brisk, minerally, dry whites are perfect for lighter appetizers such as Grilled Asparagus with Nutty Brown Butter and Sunny-Side Up Egg (page 57).

Dolchetto or Gamay Beaujolais Nouveau: Fruit-forward, light-bodied reds such as these are a nice accompaniment to heavier starters and salads with cheese. You can even serve these reds slightly chilled.

PASTA:

Fiano di Avellino or Cattaro: These indigenous Italian whites pair well with light pastas and pastas with seafood.

Chardonnay or Chablis: For heavier, cream-based pastas like Fresh Fettuccine with Mushroom Cream Sauce and Roasted Bell Peppers (page 97), try an oaky, sweet chardonnay from Napa or a French Chablis.

Malbec, shiraz, or barbera: Pastas with tomato- and meat-based sauces do well with zippy New World reds such as Argentinean malbecs, Australian Shiraz, or Italian classics grown in California, like central coast barbera.

POULTRY

Riesling, Ladera, or Sancerre: For spicy and exotic chicken dishes such as Chicken Tikka Masala (page 112), you'll need a bold, bright, and well-structured white.

Barbaresco, Pinot Noir, or Burgundy: Sauce-based, roasted, full-flavored chicken dishes can act as the perfect palate stimulus for a sophisticated, but not overbearing, red.

Pinot Noir or California Zinfandel: Everyone struggles with what to serve at Thanksgiving: red or white? I think a beautiful roast turkey offers the perfect opportunity to uncork one of these luscious reds.

SEAFOOD

Cotes du rhone or dolcetto: For heartier fish and fish soups such as New England-Style Bouillabaisse with French Bread Croutons and Rouille (page 136), try a fruit-forward French or Italian red served chilled.

Rose: I always love to pair a nice pink wine with any fish that is prepared sweet, or with a fruit garnish. A rose from coastal France or Napa is the perfect complement.

Champagne: For austere and simply prepared fish, lobster, and oysters, pop open a bottle and go for it! Don't be afraid to veer from the big houses to find value and pleasure.

MEAT

Bordeaux, Cabernet Savignon, Chianti Classico: Some of the world's boldest, most delicious wines make for the perfect accompaniment to beef. Burgundy, Pinot Noir, Napa Valley Zinfandel, and Italy's stand-out amarone are also nice pairings for red meat.

Bordeaux blanc or Gewürztraminer: These heavy whites make a nice pairing for veal, though if you prefer, you can also pair veal with a light red, such as an Oregon pinot noir.

Riesling or chinon: Like veal, pork can also be served with red or white, though I really like these full and acidic whites served with dishes such as Pork Tenderloin with Braised Fennel and Spaetzle in Orange Sauce (page 167).

DESSERT

Asti spumante: For an easy, breezy, and cheap (in the best sense of the word) dessert wine, you can always go with spumante! And if you want to skip dessert altogether in favor of a drink, try a supersweet, thick dessert wine, such as an ice wine from Canada or Germany.

BREAKFAST

STUFFED BUTTERMILK PANCAKES WITH FRESH BERRIES
AND PURE MAPLE SYRUP 26

EGG IN PURGATORY 28

EGGS BENEDICT WITH PROSCIUTTO ON CRISPY LATKES 31

EGG EN COCOTTE WITH MUSHROOMS AND BRIOCHE TOAST 35

STEAK AND EGG WITH RANCHERO SAUCE 36

CINNAMON-ORANGE FRENCH TOAST 40

BLUEBERRY SCONES WITH LEMON GLAZE 43

CRUNCHY GRANOLA 44

TROPICAL FRUIT SMOOTHIE 45

Stuffed Buttermilk Pancakes with Fresh Berries and Pure Maple Syrup

Recipe courtesy of Jenna Hamiter

Jenna, a homemaker from Texas, stands out as the only cook to prepare a sweet breakfast dish for her signature dish. The young mom cleverly uses a Danish *aebleskiver* pan to form soft popover-like pillows filled with silky sweetened cream cheese. "I make these for my three kids every weekend. They call them doughnut holes," says Jenna.

The cast-iron aebleskiver pan (see inset) resembles an egg poacher and is available at cookware stores and on the Internet.

MAKES 14

1½ cups all-purpose flour

2 tablespoons plus ¼ cup granulated sugar

2 teaspoons baking powder

½ teaspoon baking soda

¾ teaspoon kosher salt

1¼ cups buttermilk

1 large egg

3 tablespoons vegetable oil

8 ounces cream cheese, at room temperature

Zest of 1 orange, finely grated

1 teaspoon pure vanilla extract

Unsalted butter, at room temperature, for greasing the pan

1 cup mixed fresh berries

1 cup pure maple syrup

2 tablespoons confectioners' sugar

Sift the flour, 2 tablespoons granulated sugar, baking powder, baking soda, and salt into a large bowl. Make a well in the center. In a separate bowl, whisk together the buttermilk, egg, and oil. Pour into the flour mixture. Gently fold all of the ingredients together to form a moist batter. Set aside.

In the bowl of a standing electric mixer or with a handheld beater, cream together the cream cheese, orange zest, vanilla, and the ¼ cup granulated sugar. Beat for 3 minutes, or until the sugar is incorporated and the cream cheese is completely smooth.

Grease the indentations of the aebleskiver with butter and place the pan over medium heat. Spoon 1 tablespoon of the batter into each well. Carefully place 1 tablespoon of the cream cheese mixture into the mold. Top with another tablespoon of the batter to fill the mold. Cook for 2 minutes, or until the edges are set and begin to pull away from the sides of the pan. Carefully turn the pancakes over using 2 chopsticks or a fork and spoon.

Pile the pancakes on a serving platter, scatter with fresh berries, and drizzle with maple syrup. Dust with confectioners' sugar and serve immediately.

Egg in Purgatory

Recipe courtesy of Tony Carbone

Purgatory, here, is practically heaven: a chunky tomato sauce served atop a soft-cooked egg and a slice of crusty, toasted bread. Tony explained to the judges, "It's a peasant dish from southern Italy made from ingredients in a typical Italian home. It's quick and definitely hits the spot without being too heavy." Typically, the egg is poached in tomato sauce with toast served on the side. Tony says, "I wanted to reinvent the classic and make it my own by cooking the egg inside the bread, like the traditional Toad-in-a-Hole dish, and bathe it with spicy tomato sauce."

This recipe can be doubled if cooking for two.

SERVES 1

2 tablespoons extra-virgin olive oil, plus more for drizzling

½ onion, chopped (see Master the Basics: Chopping an Onion, on page 30)

1 clove garlic, minced

¼ teaspoon red-pepper flakes

Kosher salt and freshly ground black pepper

1 can (15 ounces) diced tomatoes

1 slice (¾ inch thick) brioche

1 tablespoon unsalted butter

1 large egg

1 sprig fresh flat-leaf parsley, leaves picked off the stem

2 fresh basil leaves, hand-torn

2–3 tablespoons freshly grated Parmesan cheese

Heat the oil in a small pot over medium heat. Add the onion, garlic, and red-pepper flakes. Season with salt and pepper. Cook for 5 minutes, or until the onion is softened and translucent, stirring with a wooden spoon. Stir in the tomatoes (with juice) and season again with salt and pepper. Cook, stirring occasionally, for 12 to 15 minutes, or until the sauce thickens and the flavor deepens.

Meanwhile, put the brioche on a cutting board and use a 2- to 3-inch biscuit cutter or the top of a water glass to cut out a hole in the center. Melt the butter in a small skillet over medium heat. Place the cut-out brioche round in the skillet and cook for 1 to 2 minutes per side. Set aside for serving.

Lay the remaining brioche piece in the skillet and cook for 1 to 2 minutes, or until the bottom is crisp and golden. Turn the bread over and crack the egg into the hole. Cook for 5 minutes, or until the whites are just set.

To serve, use a flat spatula to put the brioche and egg on a plate. Stir the parsley and basil leaves into the tomato sauce. Put a few spoonfuls of the sauce on top and around the plate. Sprinkle the grated Parmesan on top and drizzle with a little olive oil. Serve with the reserved brioche round for dipping.

Egg Challenge

As the top 24 amateur chefs cooked together for the first time, they took a crack at impressing the judges. In a 30-minute battle of "skill, creativity, and intuition," the judges asked that they each create a standout dish using one egg as the "hero of the dish." Judge Joe Bastianich pointed out that this deceptively simple exercise shows that while anyone can cook a soft-boiled egg, "What defines a MasterChef is what he or she does with the other 27 minutes." The contestants prepared a wide variety of egg-inspired dishes, from the runny to the remarkable. But in the end, only 14 made it through to stay in the competition.

CHOPPING AN ONION

1. Cut the onion in half, lengthwise.

2. Peel off the onion skin and discard.

3. Place the onion half face down, with the root end at the top. Slicing parallel to the chopping board, cut horizontally toward, but not through, the root, taking care at all times to keep your fingers away from the blade. Start at the base and work up, repeating two to three times.

4. Cut finely spaced vertical lines into the onion top to bottom, making sure not to cut all the way to the root.

5. Finally, chop horizontally (knife perpendicular to the cutting board) from tip to root.

Onion Chop Challenge

"If you can't chop an onion, how do you expect to put food on a plate?" That's what judge Gordon Ramsay asked the MasterChef Top 30 as a dump truck piled high with six tons of onions backed into the giant warehouse where the contestants awaited their first challenge: slicing and chopping a pile of onions with precision. "Make every cut count," Gordon told them. "Keep chopping until I say stop. When I tap you on the shoulder, you'll find out if you're making it to the next round or going home." With eyes watering and hands shaking, the contestants chopped onions for more than 90 minutes without a break. Nerves and knives proved a bloody combination for more than one contestant, as many fingers were bandaged along the way. In the end, 24 hopefuls survived the chopping block.

Eggs Benedict with Prosciutto on Crispy Latkes

Recipe courtesy of Lee Knaz

When Gordon asked the contestants to create a dish that reflected their take on a breakfast classic, Eggs Benedict, Lee knew he had to create something memorable to stay in the competition. After tasting Lee's interpretation of the dish, which included latkes (crispy potato pancakes) and prosciutto, Gordon remarked that the dish was perfectly cooked and reflected Lee's unique personality.

SERVES 4 TO 8, MAKES 8 LATKES, 1 CUP HOLLANDAISE

FOR THE LATKES

2 russet potatoes, peeled (about 1½ pounds)

1 onion

Kosher salt and freshly ground black pepper

1 large egg white

2 sprigs fresh chives, chopped, plus extra for garnish

¼ cup vegetable oil, plus more for frying

FOR THE HOLLANDAISE

1 cup (2 sticks) unsalted butter

2 large egg yolks

½ teaspoon ground coriander

Juice of ½ lemon

¼ teaspoon cayenne pepper

Kosher salt and freshly ground black pepper

FOR THE POACHED EGGS

1 tablespoon white vinegar

8 large eggs

8 slices prosciutto

Preheat the oven to 250°F.

To make the latkes: Use a box grater or food processor to coarsely grate the potatoes and onion. Put the grated potatoes and onion together in cheesecloth or a tea towel and twist it over a bowl, to squeeze out the excess liquid. Reserve the liquid. Put the dry potatoes and onions in another bowl and season with salt and pepper. Fold in the egg white and chopped chives to bind the mixture together. Spoon out the potato starch from the bottom of the potato-onion liquid and add to the grated potato mixture.

Heat a large nonstick skillet coated with the oil over medium heat. For each latke, take about 4 tablespoons of the potato mixture and press with your hands to form a pancake. Carefully drop two or three pancakes into the hot oil and gently flatten them with a spatula so they fry up thin and crispy. Fry for 3 to 4 minutes on each side, or until golden. Remove them from the pan and let them drain on several layers of paper towels. Season with salt while the latkes are still hot. Continue frying, in batches of two or three, adding more oil as needed, until all of the potato mixture is used up. Transfer all of the latkes to a baking pan and place in the warm oven.

(continued)

To make the hollandaise sauce: Melt the butter in a small pot over medium-low heat. Remove from the heat and skim and discard the white foam that rises to the surface of the butter. Carefully ladle or pour the clear golden butter into a measuring cup with a pouring spout, taking care not to add the milky solids. Set the melted butter aside.

Fill a large pot halfway with water and bring to a gentle simmer over medium heat.

In a heatproof bowl, combine the egg yolks, coriander, and 1 tablespoon of water. Whisk until the yolks are light and frothy. Put the bowl over the pot of simmering water, making sure the bottom of the bowl does not touch the water. Whisk constantly and vigorously for 2 minutes, or until the yolks are thickened and light. (If the eggs begin to scramble, or the mixture gets too hot, remove the bowl from the heat and whisk to cool).

Remove the bowl from the heat and continue whisking for a couple of minutes to cool slightly. Slowly trickle in the reserved butter as you whisk. Don't add the butter too quickly or it may curdle. When all of the butter is incorporated, whisk in the lemon juice and cayenne and season with salt and pepper. Set the bowl back over the pot of hot water (but turn off the heat) to keep it warm. Stir occasionally to prevent a skin from forming. If the sauce gets too thick, whisk in a trickle of water, 1 tablespoon at a time.

To make the poached eggs: Follow the directions on page 39.

To assemble, put a latke on each plate. Lay a slice of prosciutto on top and set a poached egg in the center. Spoon the warm hollandaise over the eggs and garnish with additional chopped chives. Serve immediately.

Egg en Cocotte with Mushrooms and Brioche Toast

Recipe courtesy of Sheena Zadeh

"When the judges announced that our challenge was to make a memorable dish with a single egg in only 30 minutes, my brain immediately thought of my favorite brunch dish, egg *en cocotte*," says Sheena. "The rich yet simple take on baked eggs is perfect for a single serving because the egg is baked in a small ramekin." When baking eggs, the objective is to have the white set but the yolk still pleasantly runny.

This recipe can be doubled if cooking for two.

SERVES 1

2 tablespoons olive oil, plus more for drizzling

1 shallot, minced

4 cremini mushrooms, wiped of grit, finely chopped

4 sprigs fresh thyme, leaves stripped from the stem and chopped (about 1 teaspoon)

Kosher salt and freshly ground black pepper

1 tablespoon dry white wine, such as Pinot Grigio

2 slices (¾ inch-thick) brioche, crusts removed

1 teaspoon unsalted butter, melted

1 large egg

2 teaspoons heavy cream

2 tablespoons (about 1 ounce) grated Gruyère or Swiss cheese

Frisée or curly endive

Preheat the oven to 400°F. In a large saucepan, bring water to a boil.

Coat a small skillet with 1 tablespoon of the oil and place it over medium heat. When the oil is hot, add the shallot. Cook, stirring, for 1 minute, or until softened. Add the mushrooms and thyme. Season with salt and pepper. Cook, stirring, for 2 to 3 minutes, or until the mushrooms lose their moisture and begin to brown. Pour in the wine and cook for 1 to 2 minutes longer, or until the liquid is completely evaporated.

Using a brush or your fingers, coat the bottom and sides of a 6-ounce ramekin with melted butter. Spoon the sautéed mushroom mixture into the ramekin, make a slight indentation in the center, and crack the egg into it. Drizzle with cream and season with salt and pepper. Sprinkle the top with a layer of cheese to cover completely. Put the ramekin in an 8 × 8-inch baking dish. Pour boiling water into the baking dish until it is halfway up the sides of the ramekin. Carefully put the baking dish in the oven. Bake for 20 minutes, or until the cheese is melted and the ramekin jiggles slightly when gently shaken.

Meanwhile, slice the brioche into ½-inch sticks. Lay them side by side on a baking pan, drizzle with some of the remaining oil, and season generously with salt and pepper. Bake for 6 minutes, or until lightly toasted and crisp.

To serve, put the ramekin in the center of a small dessert plate and stack the brioche slices on the side. Put a small mound of frisée next to the bread, drizzle with the remaining oil, and add more seasoning if desired.

Steak and Egg
with Ranchero Sauce

Recipe courtesy of Jenna Hamiter

Jenna passed the Egg Challenge with flying colors—the colors of the Texas flag, that is. She says: "Living in Dallas-Fort Worth, I know a thing or two about Tex-Mex cooking! It's the flavors I identify with most. Huevos rancheros is the ideal breakfast for me, so when the judges challenged us to cook with one egg in 30 minutes, I knew my picante tomato sauce with steak and egg would earn me a spot in the final 14."

This recipe can be doubled if cooking for two.

SERVES 1

1 tablespoon extra-virgin olive oil

2 teaspoons unsalted butter

1 clove garlic, minced

2 (2-ounce) slices skirt steak, cut ½ inch thick

Kosher salt and freshly ground black pepper

½ green bell pepper, cored, seeded, and diced

½ jalapeño chile, minced (wear plastic gloves when handling)

¼ red onion, diced

1 plum (Roma) tomato, halved, seeded, and diced

¼ teaspoon ground cumin

3 or 4 shakes of hot sauce, such as Cholula

1 large egg

½ scallion, white and green parts, thinly sliced on a bias

Coat a small skillet with half of the oil and 1 teaspoon of the butter and heat over medium-low heat. When the butter is foamy, stir in the garlic and cook for 30 seconds until fragrant, swirling the pan. Season both sides of the steak generously with salt and pepper and place the slices in the pan. Sear the steak for 3 minutes on each side, turning once. Remove the steak to a plate and set aside.

Add the remaining oil to the skillet with the meat drippings and heat to medium heat. Add the bell pepper, jalapeño, red onion, and tomato. Season with cumin, hot sauce, salt, and pepper. Cook, stirring, for 10 minutes, or until the vegetables are tender and the flavor of the sauce deepens.

Meanwhile, put another small skillet over medium heat and add the remaining 1 teaspoon butter. When the butter has melted, crack the egg into the pan, taking care to center the yolk in the white so the presentation is perfect. Don't wait too long before adding the egg. If the pan gets too hot, the edges of the egg will burn before the white is finished cooking. Cook 3 to 4 minutes, or until the white is firm and the yolk is just set. Season with salt and pepper.

To serve, spoon the ranchero sauce onto a plate. Crisscross the slices of steak on top to form an ×. Slip a flat spatula under the egg and gently set it on top of the steak. Garnish with scallion scattered on top of the egg and around the rim of the plate.

MASTER THE BASICS:

POACHING AN EGG

There are many ways to poach eggs, but the *MasterChef* method of cooking the egg first in its shell before cracking it into the water is absolutely foolproof. Cooking the egg in the shell brings it up to temperature so it will hold its shape when cracked into boiling water and the white won't feather into ragged strands. It will coagulate much faster and more evenly, which will prevent the yolk from becoming overcooked. Once you get the hang of poaching eggs, you'll find them to be one of the great secret weapons in your culinary arsenal.

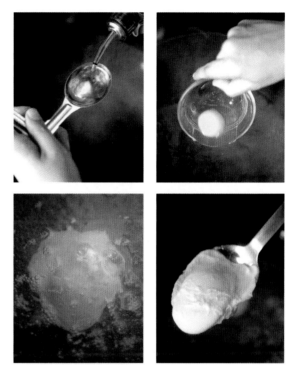

Fill a wide pot halfway with water and add a tablespoon of vinegar. Bring to a simmer over medium heat.

When the water is just barely bubbling, put the eggs, still in their shell, in the poaching water for 10 seconds.

Remove the eggs from the water. Carefully crack one egg—on a flat surface, not on the lip of a bowl—into a small cup or ladle and gently pour the egg back into the water with one continuously slow tilt. Repeat with the remaining eggs. You can easily poach two or three eggs at a time, spacing them apart in the pot.

Poach the eggs for 3 minutes, or until the whites are just cooked but the yolks are still soft.

Remove the eggs with a slotted spoon to a plate and dab the bottom of the eggs with paper towels to blot dry.

Cinnamon-Orange French Toast

 Recipe courtesy of MasterChef **Kitchen**

Is there anything better than French toast for Sunday breakfast? Thick slices of bread soaked in a rich mixture of beaten eggs and half-and-half, laced with cinnamon and vanilla, and served with fresh berries is a special weekend treat. French toast is best made with stale Italian loaf or rich brioche—fresh bread tends to get mushy and fall apart when soaked in the egg mixture.

SERVES 4

1 tablespoon ground cinnamon

1 tablespoon granulated sugar

4 large eggs

1 cup half-and-half

Zest of 1 orange, finely grated

½ teaspoon pure vanilla extract

Pinch of fine salt

8 slices (½-inch-thick) day-old
  or stale bread, such as Italian loaf
  or brioche

5 tablespoons unsalted butter

Confectioners' sugar

Maple syrup

Fresh berries

In a small bowl, mix together the cinnamon and granulated sugar. In a mixing bowl, whisk together the eggs, half-and-half, zest, vanilla, salt, and cinnamon-sugar mixture. Pour into a shallow bowl or pie plate.

Dip each slice of bread into the egg mixture, gently dragging each side along the bottom to pick up the cinnamon-sugar and zest. Allow the bread to soak for 30 seconds on each side. Whisk the egg mixture to stir up settled particles, if necessary.

In a large nonstick skillet, melt 2 tablespoons of butter over low heat. Lay 2 slices of bread in the pan at a time and cook 3 to 4 minutes per side, or until golden brown. Remove the slices from the skillet and put them in a baking pan (the pan may be placed in a warm oven, if desired). Repeat with the remaining 6 slices, adding 1 tablespoon of butter to the skillet between batches.

Serve the French toast immediately, sprinkled with confectioners' sugar and topped with maple syrup and fresh berries.

Blueberry Scones with Lemon Glaze

 Recipe courtesy of MasterChef Kitchen

This smashing recipe for the British classic quick bread is ideal for breakfast or afternoon teatime. Avoid over-mixing the batter to achieve light and airy pillows, not the hard and crumbly scones you may have had in the past. We want to eat scones, not stones! Fresh blueberries are preferable to frozen, as the color of frozen blueberries tends to bleed into the dough and spoils the look of the scone. These scones are a snap to make and never go out of style!

MAKES 2 DOZEN

FOR THE SCONES

Unsalted butter, at room temperature, for greasing the baking sheets

2 cups all-purpose flour, plus more for dusting the blueberries

1 tablespoon baking powder

½ teaspoon fine salt

2 tablespoons granulated sugar

5 tablespoons unsalted butter, cold, cut in chunks

1 cup heavy cream, plus more for brushing the scones

1 cup fresh blueberries

FOR THE GLAZE

¼ cup fresh lemon juice

1½ cups confectioners' sugar, sifted

Zest of 1 lemon, finely grated

1 tablespoon unsalted butter

Preheat the oven to 400°F. Lightly grease 2 baking sheets with butter.

To make the scones: Sift together the flour, baking powder, salt, and granulated sugar. Using 2 forks or a pastry blender, cut in the butter to coat the pieces with the flour. The mixture should look like coarse crumbs. Make a well in the center and pour in the heavy cream. Fold everything together just to incorporate. Do not overwork the dough. Toss the blueberries in some flour—to help prevent them from sinking to the bottom of the scone when baked—then fold them into the batter. Take care not to mash or bruise the blueberries because their strong color will bleed into the dough.

Using an ice cream scoop or a tablespoon, drop mounds of batter onto the prepared baking sheets, about 2 inches apart to allow for spreading. Brush the scones lightly with cream. Bake 15 to 18 minutes, or until lightly brown. Let the scones cool for at least 20 minutes before applying the glaze, or else it will not set.

To make the glaze: Mix the lemon juice and confectioners' sugar together in a microwaveable bowl. Stir until the sugar dissolves. Add the lemon zest and butter. Microwave on high power for 30 seconds. Whisk the glaze to smooth out any lumps, then drizzle the glaze over the top of the scones. Let it set for 5 minutes. Store in a covered airtight container at room temperature for up to 3 days.

Crunchy Granola

 Recipe courtesy of MasterChef Kitchen

There's no need to buy premade granola when you can whip up a quick, delicious, and low-fat batch yourself. This granola takes all of 15 minutes to prepare and combines the textures of chewy dried fruit and crunchy nuts while leaving out much of the fat and sugar found in most packaged varieties—yet it's just as addictive! Serve it sprinkled on top of yogurt and fresh fruit for a simple, healthy breakfast.

MAKES 4 CUPS

Vegetable cooking spray

2 cups rolled oats (not quick-cooking or instant)

¼ cup wheat germ

½ cup mixed nuts and seeds, such as sunflower seeds, pumpkin seeds, chopped walnuts, and almonds

¼ cup dried unsweetened shredded coconut

¼ cup honey

½ teaspoon pure vanilla extract

1 teaspoon ground cinnamon

½ teaspoon fine salt

½ cup dried cherries, cranberries, or raisins

Preheat the oven to 300°F. Coat a baking pan with cooking spray.

Combine the oats, wheat germ, nuts and seeds, and coconut. Mix with a fork to evenly distribute. Spread the oat mixture in the pan evenly. Bake for 10 to 12 minutes, or until fragrant.

Remove the baking pan from the oven. Mix in the honey, vanilla, cinnamon, and salt. Return the granola to the oven and bake for 10 to 15 minutes longer, stirring and rotating the pan halfway through cooking to prevent burning.

Remove the granola from the oven and let cool for 10 minutes to reach room temperature. Pour the granola into a large bowl or directly into an airtight container. Stir in the dried fruit. The granola will keep for 1 to 2 weeks.

Tropical Fruit Smoothie

 Recipe courtesy of MasterChef **Kitchen**

The sweet, colorful flesh of mango and papaya makes a super refreshing smoothie that is low in fat and full of flavor. A vitamin C powerhouse, this thick, tangy smoothie packs a nutritional punch, making it the perfect rejuvenator, whether enjoyed during breakfast or as a midafternoon snack. Try adding a splash of coconut milk for a colada-style shake. Here's to your day going smoothly.

SERVES 4

1 ripe mango, peeled, pitted, and cubed, about ½ cup (see Master the Basics: Cubing a Mango, on page 46)

½ cup nonfat vanilla yogurt

½ ripe papaya, peeled, seeded, and coarsely chopped, about ¾ cup (see Master the Basics: Cutting and Peeling a Papaya on page 47)

1 ripe banana, sliced

6 strawberries, stemmed and halved, about 1½ cups

Juice of ½ lime

6 ice cubes, coarsely crushed

In a blender, combine the mango and yogurt. Purée until completely liquefied. Add the papaya, banana, strawberries, lime juice, and ice. Blend until smooth and very thick, 2 to 3 minutes. Pour into chilled glasses.

CUBING A MANGO

Mangos—delicious in smoothies, luscious in salsa—can be a slimy, slippery challenge to cut. The best way to go about it is to start first with a ripe but still firm fruit. If the mango is too ripe, it will be a mushy mess and difficult to cut. A mango has one long, flat seed in the center of the fruit. Once you learn how to work around the seed, the rest is easy.

Stand the mango up on a cutting board with the stem end on the bottom. Put the knife at the top of the mango and cut down the side without hitting the seed in the center. Flip the mango around and repeat this cut on the other side.

Score the mango flesh into a grid of ½-inch cubes, being careful to cut through the flesh without piercing the skin.

Press the scored mango half inside out.

Slice off the cubes very close to the inside of the skin.

CUTTING AND PEELING A PAPAYA

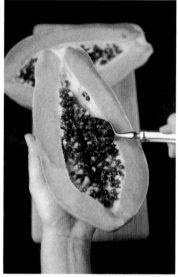

Nothing transports you to the tropics quicker than the taste of a ripe papaya. Its exotic sweet-tart flavor is wonderful in fruit salads and puréed in drinks.

The pear-shaped fruit is fairly simple to cut. Put the papaya on a cutting board. Using a chef's knife, cut the papaya in half lengthwise and separate the two pieces.

Using a tablespoon, scrape out the seeds into a bowl—papaya seeds have a peppery flavor and can be used as a substitute for black pepper in salad dressings and other recipes, if desired.

Hold the papaya cut-side down on a cutting board. Using a vegetable peeler or paring knife, peel off the papaya skin.

Cut the papaya into half moon slivers and then chop as desired.

SOUPS, SALADS & STARTERS

Duck Ssam Wraps
with Orange-Miso Sauce

Recipe courtesy of Mike Kim

Mike walked into the judging room at the very first challenge full of energy and promise. Sporting his signature hat, the waiter from Los Angeles put his heart on the plate for his signature dish, a Korean-inspired duck wrap with orange sauce. After tasting Mike's dish, Gordon Ramsay described it as "mind blowing."

Ssam, which means "wrapped" in Korean, refers to various leaf vegetables that are used to wrap a piece of bite-size meat and rice into a bundle. Mike chose supple butter lettuce leaves to cradle the rich slices of seared duck and topped it all off with bright, refreshing orange segments.

SERVES 4

1 cup short-grain rice, rinsed

2 boneless, skin-on duck breast halves

Kosher salt and freshly ground black pepper

¼ cup grapeseed oil

⅓ cup orange liqueur, such as Grand Marnier

Juice of 1 tangelo or small orange

2 teaspoons white miso paste (see Chef Ingredient: Miso, on page 52)

1 medium onion, thinly sliced

2 tablespoons rice vinegar

Juice of ½ lemon

1 teaspoon kochujang, optional (see Chef Ingredient: Kochujang, on page 52)

1 tablespoon soy sauce

1 head butter lettuce, leaves removed, rinsed, and drained

2 tangelos or small oranges, cut into segments (see Master the Basics: Segmenting Citrus, on page 53)

¼ cup pine nuts, toasted

1 tablespoon black sesame seeds, toasted

Handful of frisée

In a pot over medium-high heat, combine 2 cups of lightly salted water with the rice. Bring the rice to a boil, then reduce the heat to medium-low and cover. Simmer for 20 minutes, or until the water is absorbed and the rice is tender. Put the rice in a colander and rinse with cool water. Set aside in the sink to drain well.

Score the skin of the duck breasts in a crisscross pattern with a sharp knife, taking care not to cut all the way through the meat. Season both sides generously with salt and pepper.

Coat a large skillet with 1 tablespoon of the oil and place over medium-high heat. When the oil is hot, lay the duck breasts in the pan skin side down. Cook for 6 to 8 minutes, or until the skin is crispy and golden. As the fat renders out of the skin, carefully drain it off into a little bowl or cup—it will be used to fry the onions later.

(continued)

Turn the duck breasts over and cook for 2 minutes longer, or until firm, for medium-rare. Place the duck breasts on a cutting board and set them aside.

Remove all but 2 tablespoons of the duck fat from the skillet, reserving the rest in the bowl holding the fat that has already been drained. Return the pan to medium-high heat. Pour in the orange liqueur and cook to burn off the alcohol. Add the juice from the tangelo. Stir with a wooden spoon to scrape up the brown bits in the pan. Cook for 1 minute to reduce the liquid, then stir in the miso. Remove the orange-miso sauce from the heat and set it aside.

Put a clean skillet over medium-high heat and add 2 tablespoons of the duck fat. When the fat is sizzling, add the onion. Cook and stir for 5 minutes, or until the onion is crispy and brown, adding more duck fat if needed. Remove from the heat.

To make the vinaigrette, in a medium bowl, whisk together the vinegar, lemon juice, kochujang (if using), and soy sauce. Slowly pour in the remaining 3 tablespoons oil, continually whisking until the vinaigrette comes together. Season with salt and pepper.

To assemble the dish, slice the duck breasts. Place the lettuce leaves on a platter and spoon 2 teaspoons of rice onto each lettuce cup. Place one duck slice on top of the rice. Arrange the orange segments on top and sprinkle with the pine nuts, sesame seeds, and fried onion. Toss the frisée with the vinaigrette and put it next to the duck. Finish off by drizzling a little of the orange-miso sauce on the lettuce cups and serve the rest on the side for dipping.

CHEF INGREDIENTS:

Miso

Primarily made from fermented soybeans, miso is a thick paste that has a salty, yet subtly sweet flavor. White miso is more delicate-tasting than the darker colored varieties. Miso is becoming widely available in supermarkets and also can be purchased in Asian markets. Refrigerate after opening.

Kochujang

A popular Korean condiment, spicy *kochujang* (also spelled gochu-jang) is made from rice powder mixed with fermented soybeans and red peppers. The thick chile pepper paste is used in various Korean stews and soups and also used to marinate meat and enjoyed as a dipping sauce. Kochujang can be found in jars in the condiment aisle of Asian markets. If you cannot get kochujang in your area, you can substitute chile paste, which will not taste the same but can be used with acceptable results.

SEGMENTING CITRUS

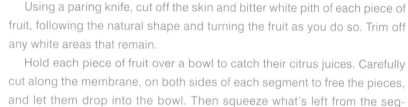

To segment an orange, lemon, lime, or grapefruit, first trim the top and bottom flat so the fruit stands steady on a work surface; cut deep enough so you see the meat of the fruit.

Using a paring knife, cut off the skin and bitter white pith of each piece of fruit, following the natural shape and turning the fruit as you do so. Trim off any white areas that remain.

Hold each piece of fruit over a bowl to catch their citrus juices. Carefully cut along the membrane, on both sides of each segment to free the pieces, and let them drop into the bowl. Then squeeze what's left from the segmented fruit over the wedges in the bowl to extract the remaining juice. Toss the segments in the juice. Remove any seeds, if necessary.

Fusion Lobster Roll with Roasted Corn Chutney and Cilantro Chimichurri

Recipe courtesy of Sharone Hakman

Sharone says, "I quit my job as a financial advisor to pursue my true passion: cooking." For his signature dish, the young dad from California made his impressive cross-cultural lobster roll, blending a sushi roll with Latin flavors. Gordon praised it as "the most ambitious dish we've seen so far. It's like you brought the United Nations onto one plate." Sharone's melding of international cuisines earned him a coveted spot in the final 14.

SERVES 2

FOR THE CHIMICHURRI

1 cup packed coarsely chopped fresh cilantro

½ cup packed coarsely chopped fresh flat-leaf parsley

¼ cup plus 1 tablespoon extra-virgin olive oil

2 cloves garlic, coarsely chopped

Juice of 2 limes, about ¼ cup

1 jalapeño chile pepper, minced (wear plastic gloves when handling)

Kosher salt and freshly ground black pepper

FOR THE CORN CHUTNEY

1 ear fresh corn on the cob, husked

½ red bell pepper, cut into ½-inch slices

1 scallion, white and green part, thinly sliced on a bias

Juice of 1 lemon

1 unripe green plantain (see Chef Ingredient: Green Plantain, on page 56)

½ cup plus 1 tablespoon vegetable oil

2 tablespoons heavy cream

FOR THE LOBSTER ROLL

¼ cup crumbled cotija cheese (see Chef Ingredient: Cotija Cheese, on page 56)

½ pound lobster tail, cooked, shelled, halved lengthwise, thinly sliced crosswise (see Master the Basics: Cracking a Lobster, on page 158)

½ ripe Hass avocado, peeled, pitted, and thinly sliced

To make the chimichurri: Combine the cilantro, parsley, ¼ cup olive oil, garlic, lime juice, and one-half of the jalapeño in a blender. Pulse until relatively smooth, stopping to scrape down the sides of the blender with a rubber spatula, if necessary. Season with salt and pepper. Pour the mixture into a small bowl and set aside at room temperature to allow the flavors to mingle. The chimichurri will keep stored in a covered container in the refrigerator for 4 to 5 days. The sauce is also great on seafood and chicken.

To make the corn chutney: Place a grill pan over medium-high heat (alternatively you may put the corn under a broiler). Place the corn and red pepper in the pan and drizzle with 1 tablespoon olive oil and season all over with salt and pepper. Char the vegetables, turning as needed, for 10 minutes, or until the pepper begins to blister and the corn kernels are slightly blackened all around and start popping. Remove from the heat. Place the peppers in a small bowl.

(continued)

Cut off the bottom of the corn and stand it upright on a cutting board. Holding the cob steady, use a sharp knife in long downward strokes to remove the kernels from the cob. Put the kernels into the bowl with the peppers and add the scallion, lemon juice, and the remaining half jalapeño. Season with salt and pepper. Toss to combine the ingredients and set aside at room temperature to let the flavors come together.

Cut off the ends of the plantain with a small, sharp knife and then cut a lengthwise slit through the peel. Cut the plantain crosswise into 1-inch-thick pieces and, beginning at the slit, pry off the peel. Place a frying pan over medium-high heat and add ½ cup vegetable oil. When the oil is hot, use tongs to gently add the plantain slices. Fry for 2 minutes on each side, or until golden brown and tender. Using tongs, transfer the fried plantains to a plate lined with paper towels to drain. Reserve the skillet with the oil.

Put the fried plantain in a food processor and add the cream, cheese, and 1 tablespoon vegetable oil, and season with salt and pepper. Blend until the mixture holds together and resembles the texture of sushi rice.

With moistened hands, spread the plantain mixture evenly onto a clean surface or wax paper. Using a flat spatula, form the mixture into two tightly packed rectangular patties, about 4 × 2 × 1 inch. Return the skillet with vegetable oil to medium-high heat. When the oil is hot, fry the patties for 2 minutes total, or until golden on all sides. Remove the fried patties to a paper towel–lined plate.

To make the lobster roll: Place the plantain on a serving plate. Alternate the sliced lobster with the sliced avocado down the length of each plantain patty. Drizzle with chimichurri and serve with the corn chutney on the side. Or, for a tasty hors d'oeuvres platter, cut the patties into 1½- to 2-inch pieces, and top each one with a slice of lobster, avocado, a tablespoon of chutney, and the chimichurri on the side for dipping.

CHEF INGREDIENTS:

Green Plantain

Commonly called a "cooking banana," this green cousin to the banana is treated like a vegetable in most dishes because it is quite starchy and has an almost squashlike flavor. Unlike bananas, plantains must be cooked before eating.

Cotija Cheese

White, salty, and crumbly, this Mexican cheese bears a resemblance in flavor and texture to feta cheese. Cotija (ko-TEE-hah) cheese is available in small rounds in the cheese section of most grocery stores or in Latin markets. If not available, feta makes a fine substitute.

Grilled Asparagus with Nutty Brown Butter and Sunny-Side Up Egg

Recipe courtesy of Graham Elliot

Graham says, "If I was confronted with the challenge of preparing a kick-ass dish featuring one egg in 30 minutes, this is what I'd make. Before you start cooking, you always want to analyze all the cooking procedures you'll need to prepare the dish. Figure out what will take the longest and start on that item first, especially when given a time constraint. This dish is rustic and elegant at the same time and makes a great starter course. Adding an egg on top of a vegetable may not seem to be an intuitive thing to do, but the egg yolk oozes onto the asparagus like a rich dressing, adding a complexity that is hard to beat."

SERVES 1

6 asparagus spears

½ cup (1 stick) unsalted butter, cut into chunks

Juice of 1 lemon

Kosher salt and freshly ground black pepper

1 tablespoon olive oil

1 large egg

1-ounce piece Pecorino cheese

Bring a pot of salted water to a boil over high heat (covering the pot will make it boil faster). Prepare an ice bath by filling a large bowl halfway with water and adding a tray of ice cubes.

Trim off the fibrous bottom of the asparagus. Blanch the asparagus in the boiling water for 30 seconds to 1 minute (they become tender very quickly). Using tongs, remove the asparagus from the water and plunge the spears into the ice bath to stop the cooking process and cool them down quickly. This also sets the vibrant green color. Once they are completely chilled, remove them from the ice bath and lay them out on paper towels to dry.

Place a small pot over medium low heat and add the butter. Cook gently, swirling the pot around, until the butter is melted. After a minute or two, the butter will foam. Stir the butter until it begins to turn brown (be especially attentive so the butter does not burn). When the butter has browned evenly, remove the pot from the heat. Add the lemon juice and season with salt and pepper. Set aside to cool.

Place a small nonstick skillet over medium heat and coat with half of the oil. Crack the egg into the pan, taking care to keep the yolk intact. Cook the egg sunny-side up for 5 minutes, or until the whites are firm but the yolk is still runny. Season with salt and pepper.

(continued)

Put a grill pan over medium-high heat. Toss the asparagus with the remaining oil and season with salt and pepper. Lay the asparagus on the hot grill and cook for 1 minute, rolling the spears around to get a nice char on all sides.

To serve, put the asparagus in the center of a small plate, set the egg on top, drizzle with the brown butter, and shave the cheese all around.

Old-School Deviled Egg

Recipe courtesy of Avis White

"Deviled Eggs fit right in with the old-school comfort foods that I love to cook and eat," says Avis. The southern grandmother's dish has a retro appeal and familiar flavors that are sure to please. She jokes, "Show up with a plate of these at a church potluck and you'll be the belle of the buffet!" Avis bear-hugged the judges when they told her she had advanced to the next round, saying, "The devil made me do it!"

SERVES 1

1 large egg, hard-boiled (see Master the Basics: The Perfect Hard-Boiled Egg on the opposite page)

1 tablespoon extra-virgin olive oil

2 cloves garlic, minced

1 teaspoon fresh lemon juice

2 tablespoons finely chopped fresh flat-leaf parsley

Kosher salt and freshly ground black pepper

1 butter lettuce leaf

1 slice tomato

1 pimiento-stuffed green olive, halved

Hard-boil the egg as directed on the opposite page.

Halve the egg lengthwise and pop out the yolk and put it in a bowl. Add the oil, garlic, lemon juice, and 1 tablespoon of the parsley. Season with salt and pepper. Mash the egg mixture with a fork until smooth.

Spoon the yolk filling into the hollowed-out egg whites.

To serve, put the lettuce leaf on a plate and the tomato slice in the center. Set the deviled egg on top and put the olive on top of each egg half. Scatter the remaining 1 tablespoon parsley around the plate.

THE PERFECT HARD-BOILED EGG

When it comes to making hard-boiled eggs, the biggest problem is that you can easily overcook them, leading to a green ring around the yolk and a rubbery texture. Here's the *MasterChef* method for cooking the perfect hard-boiled egg.

Put the egg in a pot, cover with 1 inch of cool water, and place on a stove top over medium-high heat.

Starting with cold water and gently bringing the egg to a boil will help keep it from cracking. Once the water boils, turn off the heat, cover the pot, and let the egg sit in the hot water for 10 minutes.

In the meantime, fill a large bowl with ice water. Using a strainer or slotted spoon, remove the egg from the pot of hot water and place it in the ice bath. Allow it to sit in the water for 5 minutes, or until completely cool, down to the center.

Remove the egg from the water with your fingers and give it a few gentle taps on the kitchen counter. You want to crack the shell while trying not to damage the white underneath.

Then gently roll the egg on the counter until the shell develops small cracks all over, and peel it off.

Open-Faced BLT with Fried Egg

Recipe courtesy of Whitney Miller

"The BLT is a beloved American sandwich. I wanted to make something familiar and comfortable and incorporate the egg into it," says Whitney of her Egg Challenge dish. This knife-and-fork sandwich contains the elements of a BLT—smoky bacon, crunchy bread, fresh greens, and sweet tomato—as the canvas for a soft-cooked egg. Gordon heralded it as a delicious stand-out dish with great imagination and successful execution.

SERVES 1

2 thick-cut slices bacon

1 heaping tablespoon mayonnaise

Juice and finely grated zest from
　1 lemon wedge

1 large plum (Roma) tomato, cut
　into ½-inch slices

2 tablespoons extra-virgin olive oil

1 clove garlic, minced

Kosher salt and freshly ground
　black pepper

2 teaspoons unsalted butter

1 slice (½ inch thick) sourdough
　baguette

1 large egg

1 small handful baby spinach
　leaves

4 fresh basil leaves, hand-torn

Preheat the oven to 375°F.

Put a skillet over medium heat. Fry the bacon for 5 minutes total, or until crispy on both sides. Drain the bacon on a plate lined with paper towel. Set the skillet aside with the bacon grease.

In a small bowl, combine the mayonnaise with the lemon zest and juice. Set aside in the refrigerator.

Put the tomato slices side by side in an 8 × 8-inch baking dish, drizzle with oil, sprinkle with garlic, and season with salt and pepper. Bake for 8 minutes, or until the tomatoes are slightly softened and fragrant. Spread 1 teaspoon of the butter on the bread and put the slice in the oven during the last 4 minutes of baking the tomatoes, until lightly browned.

Return the bacon skillet to medium heat and add the remaining 1 teaspoon butter. When the butter is foamy, crack the egg into a ramekin and carefully pour it into the pan. Cook for 2 to 3 minutes, or until the white is set. Season with salt and pepper.

To serve, spread the mayonnaise evenly on one side of the bread. Put the bread on a plate, lay the bacon across it, and layer the tomatoes in an overlapping pattern on top. Scatter the spinach on top and put the egg in the center. Garnish with basil.

Pan-Fried Rice Noodle Pancake with Egg Roll (Pho Ap Chao Hot Ga Cuon)

Recipe courtesy of Slim Huynh

"When the judges said they wanted an innovative dish featuring a single egg, I wanted to go for it!" says Slim. Her crispy fried noodle egg roll impressed judge Joe Bastianich. "That's probably one of the more ambitious dishes we've seen," he observed. Slim's ambition ultimately earned her a spot in the final 14. "I'm putting my four-year education aside," she told the judges. "*MasterChef* is my dream!"

SERVES 1

½ pound dried rice noodles/sticks (see Chef Ingredient: Dried Rice Noodles on the opposite page)

3 tablespoons vegetable oil

1 clove garlic, slivered

Kosher salt and freshly ground black pepper

1 large egg

1 shallot, minced

Pinch of sugar

4 thin slices plum (Roma) tomato

4 sprigs fresh cilantro, finely chopped

4 fresh basil leaves, finely chopped

4 fresh chives

2 tablespoons soy sauce

Juice of ½ lime

2 teaspoons Sriracha (see Chef Ingredient: Sriracha Chile Sauce, on page 108)

Put the noodles in a bowl and cover with warm water (never use boiling water to soften dried rice sticks, because they will become mushy). Soak for 15 to 20 minutes, or until the noodles are pliable. Drain the noodles and dry completely with paper towels.

Coat a 10-inch skillet with 2 tablespoons of the oil and place over medium-high heat. When the oil is hot, add the garlic and stir for a few seconds, until fragrant. Lay the noodles in the pan and spread them out so they cover the entire bottom in an even layer. Season with salt and pepper. Press the noodles down with the back of a flat spatula to create a rice noodle pancake. Continue to cook, pressing down, for 5 minutes, or until the noodles are flat and crisp. Turn the noodle pancake over, reduce the heat to medium, and cook for 2 minutes, or until crisp. Set aside.

In a small bowl, whisk the egg with the shallot and sugar. Season with salt and pepper. Coat a small nonstick skillet with the remaining 1 tablespoon oil and place over medium-low heat. When the oil is hot, add the egg mixture. Swirl the pan around over the flame to cover the bottom completely. Put the pan back on the stove and gently cook for 3 minutes, or until the egg is set in a round disk.

To assemble, lay a large piece of plastic wrap or a sushi mat on a work surface. Put the rice noodle pancake on the plastic close to you. Set the egg on top of the pancake. Layer the tomatoes in an overlapping pattern on top of the egg, scatter the cilantro and basil, and season with salt and pepper. Using the plastic wrap, carefully tuck and roll up the pancake away from you into a log. Remove the plastic wrap. Tie the chives at intervals around the egg roll to hold it together.

Make a quick dipping sauce by combining the soy, lime juice, and Sriracha in a small bowl.

To serve, cut the egg roll in between the chives into 1½-inch pieces. Serve the dipping sauce on the side.

Dried Rice Noodles

Often called pad thai noodles or rice vermicelli, these translucent, fragile sticks are made from rice and typically come dried. They're basically flavorless but will absorb the seasonings of any sauce or soup that surrounds them. Unlike pasta, rice noodles are not boiled but soaked in water, as boiling makes them mushy. The softened noodles have a wonderful chewy, but tender texture. Rice noodles come in a variety of sizes. Buy the ones that look like flat fettuccine. They are available in nearly any Asian market and in many grocery stores.

Chinese Egg Rolls with Sweet and Sour Mandarin Sauce

Recipe courtesy of Sheetal Bhagat

Sheetal says, "When the judges announced that our challenge was to create a Chinese dish highlighting mandarin oranges, my mind went completely blank. I typically cook Indian cuisine, so Asian dishes are out of my comfort zone. In Calcutta, street vendors sell *kati rolls*, a spicy mixture of meat and vegetables rolled in Indian flatbread and fried until crispy. The tangy mandarin dipping sauce also makes for a terrific glaze brushed on shrimp."

SERVES 4, MAKES 12 ROLLS AND ½ CUP SAUCE

6 tablespoons peanut oil

2 cloves garlic, minced

1 tablespoon grated fresh ginger

1 scallion, white and light green parts, finely chopped

2 (4-ounce) bone-in chicken thighs, meat chopped into ½-inch pieces, skin and bones discarded

Kosher salt and freshly ground black pepper

1 small head baby bok choy, finely shredded

1 tablespoon rice vinegar

4 teaspoons soy sauce

1 tablespoon sesame oil

½ teaspoon cornstarch

½ teaspoon sugar

Segments and juice of 1 mandarin orange (see Master the Basics: Segmenting Citrus, on page 53)

2 tablespoons honey

2 tablespoons white vinegar

2 teaspoons mirin (see Chef Ingredient: Mirin, on the opposite page)

¼ teaspoon red-pepper flakes

12 square wonton wrappers

To make the filling, coat a wok or large skillet with 2 tablespoons of the peanut oil and place over medium-low heat. When the oil is hot, add the garlic, ginger, and scallion and stir for 30 seconds, or until fragrant, taking care not to burn them. Increase the heat to medium, add the chicken, season with salt and pepper, and stir-fry for 6 to 7 minutes, or until no longer pink. Add the bok choy and stir-fry for 1 minute, or until softened. Add the rice vinegar, soy sauce, and sesame oil. Sprinkle in the cornstarch and sugar, stirring to dissolve. Continue to stir-fry the chicken mixture for another minute.

Remove the filling to a plate and spread out to cool. You should have about 2 cups. Prop up one end of the plate so that it tilts, allowing the juices to drain to one end (all of that excess liquid will make the egg roll soggy). Discard the juices. Let the filling cool for 10 minutes.

To make the mandarin dipping sauce, combine the orange juice and segments, honey, white vinegar, mirin, and red-pepper flakes in a blender. Pulse to combine. Season with salt and pepper.

To fill the egg rolls, lay a wonton wrapper on a work surface with the pointed corner at the top, so it looks like a diamond. Put about 1 tablespoon of the chicken filling on one corner. Roll the corner closest to you over the filling. Brush the top corner with water. Fold in the sides of the wonton and continue rolling the egg roll up until it is closed. Press to seal and set aside, seam side down. Continue with the remaining wontons.

To fry the egg rolls, coat a skillet with the remaining 4 tablespoons peanut oil and place over medium heat. When the oil is hot, lay 4 egg rolls in the pan and fry for 4 to 6 minutes, turning, until golden on all sides. Remove the fried egg rolls to a wire rack to drain and cool. Serve with the mandarin sauce on the side for dipping.

CHEF INGREDIENT:

Mirin

Characterized by a sweet taste and low alcohol content, mirin is a popular Japanese rice wine used for cooking. Mirin adds a bright and fragrant aroma to dishes and is widely available.

CRACKING A DUNGENESS CRAB

When purchasing live crabs, be sure they are moving around and active. After you purchase them, keep crabs refrigerated and use within two or three days for optimum flavor.

When cracking a cooked crab, be prepared to make a mess—wear an apron and rubber gloves, if you choose! For delicious crab stock, save the shells and boil them later with carrot, celery, and onion.

1. Pick up the crab and, holding the body, twist off the claws and legs.

2. Holding the crab belly side up, pull off the triangular-shaped belly flap, or apron.

3. Turn over the crab and remove the top shell by inserting your thumb between the body and the shell at the rear of the crab and pulling it up and off.

4. With the top shell removed, break off the hard mouth of the crab. Gently scrape away the colored connective tissue and the fingerlike gills surrounding the body. Rinse the body under cold water.

5. Pick out meat from the body carefully, in whole pieces.

6. Using a nutcracker or hammer, crack open the legs and claws and carefully pull out the meat.

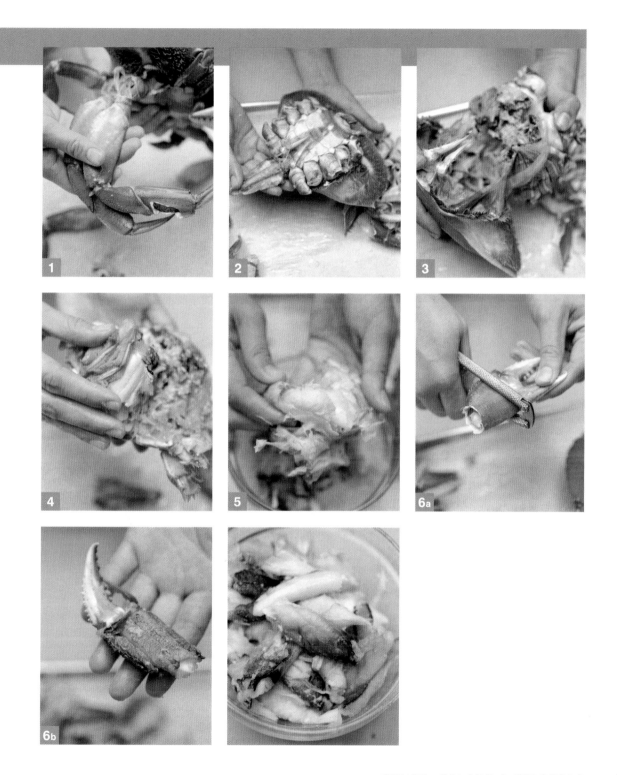

Dungeness Crab Salad with Fresh Avocado and Gazpacho Andalouse Sauce

Recipe courtesy of Lee Knaz

"This was my first Mystery Box win, and I was pretty surprised that the judges picked it," says Lee. "I'd never cooked a live crab before. This dish was a real turning point in the competition for me. Prior to this, I had a habit of coming in under the radar. When Joe tasted the sweet crab salad floating in a pool of refreshing gazpacho, he slammed the table and said, 'BAM! Now you're talking. The flavors are action on your palate! Clean, focused—it's a first-rate dish.' To hear the judges tell me this was among the best dishes they'd tasted in the competition was just amazing.

If cooking fresh or live whole crabs is not your thing, feel free to substitute lump crabmeat. But whatever you do, do not use that imitation stuff.

SERVES 4

FOR THE CRAB SALAD

- 1 (2-pound) live Dungeness crab or ½ pound lump crabmeat, picked through for shells (see Master the Basics: Cracking a Dungeness Crab, on page 68)
- 1 onion, cut into chunks
- 1 garlic head, halved
- 1 carrot, cut into chunks
- 2 celery stalks, cut into chunks
- ½ bunch fresh flat-leaf parsley
- ½ bunch fresh basil
- 1 cup dry white wine, such as Sauvignon Blanc
- 1 teaspoon whole black peppercorns
- 1 shallot, minced
- 1 teaspoon mustard seeds, toasted (see Master the Basics: Toasting Spices, on page 73)

- 1 teaspoon fennel seeds, toasted (see Master the Basics: Toasting Spices)
- 2 thin slices prosciutto, chopped
- ½ Granny Smith apple, peeled, cored, and finely diced
- 1 bunch thin asparagus, ends trimmed, finely chopped, tips reserved
- ½ English cucumber, peeled, seeded, and finely diced
- 2 tablespoons extra-virgin olive oil, plus more for drizzling
- Juice of 1 lemon
- Kosher salt and freshly ground black pepper
- ½ ripe Hass avocado, pitted, peeled, and cut into ½-inch slices for garnish

FOR THE GAZPACHO

- 2 large vine-ripe tomatoes, seeded and coarsely chopped (see Master the Basics: Seeding a Tomato, on page 73)
- ½ onion, coarsely chopped
- ½ English cucumber, coarsely chopped
- ½ red or yellow bell pepper, cored, seeded, and coarsely chopped
- 1 clove garlic, minced
- Juice of ½ lemon
- 1½ teaspoons sugar
- 1 teaspoon smoked paprika
- Kosher salt and freshly ground black pepper
- ½ cup extra-virgin olive oil

(continued)

To make the crab salad: If using live crab, put it in the freezer for 20 minutes before cooking so that it is easier to handle. Put a large pot of well-salted water over medium-high heat. Add the aromatics—the onion, garlic, carrot, celery, parsley, basil, wine, and peppercorns. Bring the water to a rolling boil and carefully submerge the crab in the water. Cover the pot to bring the water quickly back up to a boil. Cook the crab for 12 to 15 minutes. The shell should turn bright red.

Put the crab in a bowl of ice water for several minutes to cool completely. Clean and crack the crab as directed on page 44.

Combine the shallot, mustard and fennel seeds, prosciutto, apple, asparagus, cucumber, oil, and lemon juice in a mixing bowl. Add the crab body meat, about 1½ cups. Reserve the claw meat for garnish. Gently fold the ingredients together, taking care not to break up the crabmeat too much. Season with salt and pepper. Set aside in the refrigerator to marinate for 5 to 10 minutes while you make the gazpacho.

To make the gazpacho: Combine the tomatoes, onion, cucumber, bell pepper, garlic, lemon juice, sugar, paprika, salt, and pepper in a blender. Purée until smooth. With the motor running, drizzle in the oil. Strain the gazpacho through a fine-mesh strainer into a bowl, pressing the solids with a wooden spoon to extract as much liquid as possible.

To serve, set a 3-inch ring mold in the center of a shallow bowl or plate. Fill the ring with the crab salad, pressing down gently with the back of a spoon to pack. Ladle a pool of the gazpacho around the ring to cover the bowl. Carefully remove the ring. Repeat with the 3 remaining servings. Garnish the crab salad with whole claw meat, asparagus tips, and a few slices of avocado. Drizzle the plate with oil and season with salt and pepper before serving.

SEEDING A TOMATO

The seeds of a tomato can sometimes lend a bitter taste to a dish and can actually add more water to a recipe than necessary. Removing the seeds will lead to not only a better taste but also a more even texture in your dish.

Cut the tomato in half at the equator (crosswise). Turn the tomato cut side down and gently squeeze out the seeds or push them out with your fingers. Chop or slice seeded tomatoes as desired.

TOASTING SPICES

When spices are toasted, their flavors intensify, adding a deeper dimension to your food.

Put spices in a dry skillet and place over medium-low heat. Toast for just a minute or two to release the fragrant oils, shaking the pan so the spices don't scorch.

Caesar Salad

 Recipe courtesy of MasterChef Kitchen

For one of the Field Challenges, the contestants were split into teams and thrown into a professional kitchen. Their task: to cater a wedding feast for 230 guests. Caesar salad was served as the first course.

The essentials of a well-prepared Caesar salad are wonderfully simple: crisp lettuce, real Parmesan, and a dressing brightly flavored with garlic, lemon, and anchovy. Freshness of all components is critical. Showcase this versatile salad as the base for an array of proteins—grilled chicken, steak, or shrimp—or tucked into a wrap for a light lunch.

SERVES 4, MAKES 1 CUP DRESSING

FOR THE CROUTONS

1 loaf (8 ounces) rustic Italian bread, crusts removed, cut into ¾-inch cubes

2 tablespoons extra-virgin olive oil

2 teaspoons kosher salt

½ teaspoon freshly ground black pepper

¼ teaspoon cayenne pepper

FOR THE DRESSING

4 cloves garlic, minced

2 anchovy fillets, rinsed and minced

1 large egg yolk

1 teaspoon Dijon mustard

Juice of 1 lemon

1 teaspoon red wine vinegar

½ teaspoon Worcestershire sauce

Kosher salt and freshly ground black pepper

½ cup extra-virgin olive oil

FOR THE SALAD

2 heads romaine lettuce, inner leaves only

1 cup freshly grated Parmesan cheese

To make the croutons: Preheat the oven to 400°F.

Put the bread cubes in a large bowl, drizzle with the oil, and toss until coated. Sprinkle the salt, black pepper, and cayenne over the bread cubes, and toss until evenly coated. Spread the bread cubes on a baking pan in a single layer. Bake for 10 minutes, or until the croutons are golden. The croutons should be crisp but not too hard to pierce with a fork. Set aside to cool.

To make the dressing: Combine the garlic, anchovies, egg yolk, mustard, lemon juice, vinegar, and Worcestershire in a small bowl. Season with salt and pepper. Use a small whisk or a fork to mix the ingredients thoroughly until smooth. Gradually whisk in the oil in a slow, steady stream, until the dressing is thick.

To make the salad: Tear the lettuce into a large salad bowl and add the croutons. Add enough dressing to coat the salad to your liking and mix gently. Add the Parmesan and toss the salad well to evenly distribute. Serve immediately.

Wedge Salad Smothered with Blue Cheese

 Recipe courtesy of MasterChef Kitchen

Nothing kicks off a juicy steak dinner better than a classic wedge salad drizzled with blue cheese. The creamy dressing and crispy lettuce gives comfort food an air of rich indulgence. The bold, sharp dressing is a cinch to make and is also terrific with chicken wings or as a dip for fresh vegetables.

SERVES 4, MAKES 1¼ CUPS DRESSING

½ cup sour cream

¼ cup mayonnaise

2 tablespoons buttermilk

2 tablespoons red wine vinegar

Pinch of sugar

½ teaspoon freshly ground black pepper

¾ cup crumbled blue cheese, preferably Roquefort (see Chef Ingredient: Roquefort Blue Cheese below)

1 head iceberg lettuce

1 tomato, diced

¼ small red onion, finely diced

4 slices bacon, fried and crumbled

In a large mixing bowl, whisk together the sour cream, mayonnaise, and buttermilk. Add the vinegar, sugar, and pepper. Whisk until well-mixed. Add the blue cheese to the bowl, reserving some for garnishing the salad, and gently fold in using a rubber spatula. Transfer the dressing to a covered storage container and refrigerate for at least 1 hour and up to 2 days.

Remove any wilted outside leaves from the head of lettuce. Hit the bottom of the head on a flat surface to loosen the core. Pull the core out with your fingers. Cut the lettuce head into quarters.

Build the salad by placing 1 lettuce wedge on each of 4 plates facing up. Drizzle equal amounts of dressing over each wedge. Scatter the tomato, onion, bacon, and reserved blue cheese over each salad.

CHEF INGREDIENT:

Roquefort Blue Cheese

Named after a village in the south of France, Roquefort is especially known for its pungent smell and characteristic blue-green veins of mold. This crumbly sheep's milk cheese is sold in rough wedges and has a sharp, salty tang and creamy-moist texture.

New England Clam Chowder

Recipe courtesy of Dave Miller

"Being from Boston, I know a thing or two about clam chowder," says Dave. "When the judges challenged us to make it for them, I was thrilled! This Boston clam chowder recipe is hearty and rich—when you're craving some delicious comfort food, it really hits the spot!"

SERVES 6

2 dozen large cherrystone clams, scrubbed and rinsed

1 bottle (750 ml) plus ¼ cup dry white wine, such as Pinot Grigio

6 bacon slices, cut into ½-inch strips

2 tablespoons unsalted butter

1 onion, chopped

2 celery stalks, chopped

Kosher salt and freshly ground black pepper

4 sprigs fresh thyme

Pinch of red-pepper flakes

2 bay leaves

2 cups potatoes, peeled and cut into 1-inch cubes

2 cups heavy cream

1 cup whole milk

1 tablespoon extra-virgin olive oil

Oyster crackers or crusty bread

Put the clams in a large soup pot over medium-high heat. Pour in the bottle of wine and 2 cups of water. Bring to a simmer, cover the pot, and steam for 5 to 10 minutes, or until the clams open. Discard any clams that do not open.

Transfer the clams to a large bowl to cool. Strain the broth through a fine-mesh sieve lined with cheesecloth to remove any grit. When the clams are cool enough to handle, remove them from their shells and chop into ½-inch pieces. Set the clams and broth aside.

Return the pot to medium heat. Add the bacon and fry until crisp and the fat is rendered. Add the butter, onion, and celery and season with salt and pepper. Cook and stir for 3 to 5 minutes, or until the vegetables are slightly softened. Add the ¼ cup wine and continue to cook until the liquid has evaporated. Stir in the thyme, red-pepper flakes, and bay leaves. Continue to cook and stir for 5 minutes, or until the vegetables are completely tender.

Add the potatoes and reserved clam broth and bring to a boil. Reduce the heat to medium-low, cover, and simmer for 30 minutes, or until the broth thickens slightly and the potatoes are very tender. (If you like a thicker broth, mash some of the potatoes against the side of the pot with a wooden spoon.) Remove from the heat. Discard the thyme stems and bay leaves. Stir in the clams, cream, and milk and season again with salt and pepper.

Ladle the chowder into soup bowls and top each with a few drops of olive oil. Serve with oyster crackers or crusty bread.

Minestrone Soup with Escarole

 Recipe courtesy of MasterChef **Kitchen**

This rustic soup is a meal in itself. Minestrone means "big soup" in Italian. For a vegetarian option, feel free to omit the pancetta. Seasoning with salt and pepper in stages is imperative to capture the layers of flavor.

SERVES 8

3 tablespoons olive oil

2 ounces pancetta, chopped, about ⅓ cup (see Chef Ingredient: Pancetta below)

1 onion, chopped

1 carrot, chopped

1 celery stalk, chopped

4 cloves garlic, chopped

1 leek, white and light green parts, cleaned and chopped (see Master the Basics: Cleaning Leeks, on page 83)

2 bay leaves

Kosher salt and freshly ground black pepper

½ pound escarole, cleaned and shredded (see Chef Ingredients: Escarole, on page 82)

1 can (28 ounces) whole tomatoes, with juice

1 quart Vegetable Broth (page 243) or store-bought

1 cup farro, rinsed (see Chef Ingredients: Farro, on page 82)

1 can (15 ounces) white beans, rinsed and drained

6 fresh basil leaves, chopped

Freshly grated Parmesan cheese

Coat a soup pot with 2 tablespoons of the oil and place over medium heat. When the oil is hot, add the pancetta. Cook and stir for 1 minute to render some of the fat. Add the onion, carrot, celery, garlic, leek, and bay leaves. Season with a generous amount of salt and pepper. Cook and stir for 10 minutes, or until the vegetables are softened. Add the escarole and continue to cook, folding the leaves over, until slightly wilted.

Add the tomatoes and break them up with a wooden spoon into bite-sized pieces. Cook and stir for 5 minutes. Season again with salt and pepper. Pour in the broth and bring the soup to a boil. Simmer for 20 to 25 minutes, stirring occasionally.

Meanwhile, bring 2 cups of lightly salted water to a boil over high heat. Add the farro, cover the pot, and reduce the heat to medium-low. Simmer for 20 minutes, or until the water is absorbed and the farro has a chewy, tender texture. Drain well and rinse with cool water.

In a nonstick skillet, heat the remaining 1 tablespoon oil. Add the farro and cook over medium-high heat for 5 minutes, or until toasty and golden.

Stir the farro, beans, and basil into the soup. Simmer for 5 to 10 minutes to heat the beans through. Ladle the soup into bowls, sprinkle each with cheese, and serve.

CHEF INGREDIENT:

Pancetta

Pancetta is the Italian equivalent of bacon. It is cured with salt, pepper, and other spices but is not smoked like American bacon. Pancetta adds a distinctive pork flavor to pasta and other dishes, without infusing the smokiness of bacon. It is generally sold rolled up into a cylinder shape and is available at meat markets, some supermarkets, and Italian grocers.

Farro

A wheatlike grain popular during the golden days of old Rome, farro is enjoying renewed popularity in restaurants across the country. Farro looks like a plumper version of barley and has an earthy, nutty flavor and firm, chewy texture. It is available in most grocery stores.

Escarole

A wonderfully versatile green, Joe says that escarole is "one of those vegetables that people aren't sure how to prepare. You can eat escarole raw in salad, but I think it's best cooked. It's less bitter than its cousins, radicchio and chicory, and sautéing mellows out the flavor, making it sweet and vibrant."

Before using escarole in a recipe, it needs to be thoroughly washed. Simply submerge escarole leaves in a bowl of cold water, swish around, remove, and pat dry.

CLEANING LEEKS

Leeks are a favorite vegetable of the pros because they have a more delicate and sweeter flavor than onions and add a subtle touch to recipes without overpowering other flavors.

Cut off the bottom root portion and dark green tops and discard.

Cut the leeks lengthwise and run under cold water. Separate the leek pieces, checking for dirt between the layers.

Allow leeks to air dry or pat dry with a kitchen towel. Chop as desired.

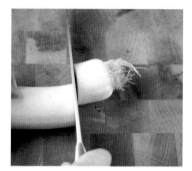

Caramelized Onion Dip with Potato Chips

 Recipe courtesy of MasterChef **Kitchen**

A rich, creamy dip is a must-have for any good party. Caramelizing onions does take a little time, but this recipe is a thousand times better than ripping open a packet of dried soup and mixing it with sour cream. Make the onion dip ahead of time so the flavors can blend and mellow. If you want to bump the flavor up to the next level, add a little crumbled bacon. This dip is the perfect accompaniment to crudités or pita chips and is also delicious spread on a burger.

For a healthier option, you can substitute Greek-style yogurt for the cream cheese. The end result will not be as thick but will still be rich with flavor.

MAKES ABOUT 2 CUPS

2 tablespoons extra-virgin olive oil

1 tablespoon unsalted butter

2 large onions, thinly sliced (about 1½ pounds)

½ teaspoon kosher salt, plus more for seasoning

¼ teaspoon freshly ground black pepper, plus more for seasoning

4 ounces cream cheese, very soft

½ cup sour cream

½ cup Best Mayonnaise (see page 246) or quality store-bought

Chopped fresh chives, for garnish

Thick-cut salt and pepper potato chips, store-bought

Add the oil and butter to a large skillet and place over medium heat. When the butter has melted, add the onions, salt, and pepper. Stir occasionally and cook for 20 minutes, or until the onions are deeply golden brown and caramelized. Watch carefully so as not to allow the onions to burn. Remove the onions from the heat and set aside for 15 minutes, or until completely cooled.

In a large bowl using a handheld electric mixer, beat the cream cheese on low speed for 1 minute, just until smooth and free of any lumps. Mix in the sour cream and mayonnaise. Fold in the caramelized onions with all their juices and season again with salt and pepper, if needed. Refrigerate for at least 2 hours or up to 2 days. If the dip is made a day or two in advance, store it covered in the refrigerator and simply bring it to room temperature before serving. Garnish with chopped chives and serve with potato chips.

Baked Brie with Blackberry Sauce

 Recipe courtesy of MasterChef **Kitchen**

Baked Brie is an easy and elegant crowd-pleaser that should be part of everyone's party-food repertoire. Spooning a tart blackberry sauce over the smooth, gooey Brie intensifies the flavor of the cheese and makes the presentation even more stunning. For the best texture, let the Brie cool slightly before topping it with the blackberry sauce.

SERVES 8, MAKES 1 CUP SAUCE

1 wheel (8 ounces, 4 inches) Brie cheese (see Chef Ingredient: Brie on the opposite page)

½ cup slivered almonds

1 sheet (11 × 17 inches) frozen puff pastry, thawed

3 tablespoons whole milk

1 tablespoon unsalted butter

1 pint fresh blackberries or thawed frozen whole blackberries, if fresh are not available

1 fresh vanilla bean, split lengthwise

1 tablespoon honey

¼ cup brandy (optional)

Pinch of salt

Juice of ½ lemon

Sliced baguette and water crackers

Preheat the oven to 400°F. Coat a baking pan with vegetable oil cooking spray.

Using a long sharp knife, carefully cut the wheel of Brie in half horizontally through the middle, placing your hand on top of the wheel to steady it as you turn it around to make an even slice. Gently pry the two pieces of Brie apart and open it up like a sandwich. Sprinkle the almonds on the cut side of one layer of cheese. Place the top circle of Brie on top of the almonds, cut side down, and press down gently.

On a lightly floured surface, roll the pastry with a rolling pin to smooth out the seams and make the sheet a little bigger. Using a sharp knife, cut the corners off the pastry to form a rounder shape. Put the Brie in the center of the pastry and gather up the sides to make a parcel. Decoratively twist and pinch the ends together to seal the pastry. Brush with milk.

Carefully transfer the Brie to the baking pan. Bake for 20 minutes, or until the pastry is evenly puffed and browned.

Meanwhile, prepare the blackberry sauce. Melt the butter in a pot over medium-low heat. When the butter is foamy, add the blackberries and gently toss them to coat in the butter, but take care not to mash them up too much. Scrape the seeds from the vanilla bean and add to the blackberries, along with the pod for extra flavor. Add the honey and brandy (if using). Raise the heat to medium and cook for 15 to 20 minutes, or until the berries are soft but remain intact and the liquid thickens slightly.

Remove the pot from the heat and sprinkle with a pinch of salt and a squeeze of lemon juice to balance out the sweetness of the sauce. Remove the vanilla pod and discard. Set the blackberry sauce aside to cool slightly and thicken.

Carefully transfer the baked Brie to a decorative platter. Allow it to cool for a minute or two. Spoon the blackberry sauce on top of the Brie. Serve it warm or at room temperature with sliced baguette and crackers.

CHEF INGREDIENT:

Brie

With a thin, edible white rind and a sinfully buttery center, Brie is one of the most beloved cheeses in the world. Mild and slightly sweet in flavor, Brie is a soft young cheese usually made from cow's milk. The moldy exterior is edible and adds a toothsome quality to the supple center. Brie is sold in most supermarkets and is best served at room temperature or warmed; it pairs well with fruit.

PASTA

Faruq

Chic Macaroni and Cheese

Recipe courtesy of Faruq Jenkins

For his signature dish, Faruq re-created his grandmother's recipe for supersatisfying cheesy goodness. "I wanted to put my own spin on my 80-year-old grandmother's beloved macaroni and cheese while honoring her at the same time," Faruq says.

Gordon Ramsay issued him a warning: "If you're going to bring us mac and cheese, make sure it's the best." Ultimately, Gordon was impressed—and praised Faruq's crisp and flavorful bacon-crumb topping with soft, velvety pasta in cheese sauce bubbling below.

SERVES 6

½ cup (1 stick) unsalted butter, at room temperature, plus extra for greasing pan

1 can (12 ounces) evaporated milk

2 cups shredded sharp white Cheddar cheese

Pinch of cayenne pepper

3 large eggs

1½ cups dry elbow macaroni, cooked al dente and drained

Kosher salt and freshly ground black pepper

2 cups shredded fontina cheese

1½ cups cubed Havarti cheese

6 bacon strips

1 cup panko (Japanese) bread crumbs

½ cup grated Parmesan cheese

Preheat the oven to 375°F. Using the additional softened butter, grease the bottom and sides of a 10 × 8-inch baking dish.

In a pot over medium-low heat, combine the ½ cup of butter, evaporated milk, and Cheddar. Sprinkle in the cayenne and gently simmer, stirring occasionally, for 6 to 8 minutes, or until the mixture thickens into a creamy cheese sauce.

In a large mixing bowl, whisk the eggs until foamy. Add the cooked macaroni and mix to coat the noodles evenly. Season with salt and pepper. Slowly pour in the hot cheese sauce, stirring to combine. Add the fontina and Havarti cheeses and toss to evenly distribute.

Pour the mixture into the prepared baking dish. Bake for 20 to 25 minutes, or until the cheese starts to bubble and thicken.

Meanwhile, place a skillet over medium-low heat. When the pan is hot, add the bacon and fry for 5 minutes, or until crisp on both sides. Remove the bacon to a plate lined with paper towel.

When it has cooled, crumble the bacon into a bowl and add the bread crumbs and Parmesan.

Remove the mac and cheese from the oven and sprinkle the top with the bacon bread crumbs. Bake for 8 to 10 minutes longer, or until lightly toasted golden brown. Cool for 5 minutes.

For a great presentation, punch out a piece of the mac and cheese with a round 3-inch biscuit cutter.

Homemade Pasta

Recipe courtesy of Joe Bastianich

For the Pasta Pressure Test, the contestants were charged with the task of creating a stellar pasta dish to save them from elimination. Judge Joe Bastianich, one of America's foremost authorities on regional Italian cuisine, set up the challenge with a bold statement: "There are two kinds of people in the world: Italians and people who want to be Italian." When executed properly, Joe's recipe for homemade pasta can make almost anyone into an authentic Italian cook!

MAKES 1 POUND

3 cups unbleached all-purpose flour, plus more for dusting

4 large eggs

1 teaspoon extra-virgin olive oil

1 teaspoon kosher salt

Cornmeal (optional)

Mound the flour in the center of a large wooden cutting board. Make a well in the center of the flour, like a volcano. In a small bowl, beat the eggs, oil, and salt together until the eggs are foamy. Pour into the flour well.

Using a fork, beat the egg mixture while slowly incorporating the flour from the sides of the crater into the egg mixture. Continue beating until the dough becomes too stiff to mix with a fork. The dough will come together in a shaggy mass.

Start kneading the dough with both hands, primarily using the palms of your hands. If the dough is too sticky, add more flour, a little at a time. If the dough is too dry, add a teaspoon of water.

Once the dough is a cohesive mass, sprinkle a little flour on top. Knead the dough by gathering it into a compact ball, then pushing the ball away from you with the heels of your hands. Repeat the gathering-

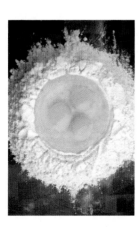

and-pushing motion several times, and then press into the dough, first with the knuckles of one hand, then with the other, several times. Alternate between kneading and "knuckling" the dough until it is smooth, silky, and elastic—it pulls back into shape when you stretch it. The process will require about 10 minutes of constant kneading, essential for light pasta dough.

Flour the work surface and your hands lightly anytime the dough begins to stick while you're kneading. Form the dough into a smooth ball and place in a small bowl. Cover with plastic wrap and let the dough rest at least 30 minutes before rolling and shaping the pasta.

Cut the rested dough into 4 equal pieces. Working with one piece at a time (cover the pieces you are not using to prevent them from drying out), roll or hand-press the pasta out on a lightly floured surface into a rectangle. Roll the dough through the pasta machine, two or three times, at the widest setting. Pull and stretch the sheet of dough with the palm of your hand as it emerges from the rollers. Reduce the setting and crank the dough through again, two or three times. Continue tightening until the machine is at the narrowest setting. The dough should be paper-thin, about ¼ inch thick—you should be able to see your hand through it. Dust the sheets of dough with flour as needed. The dough can be cut as desired.

Cut the long sheet of pasta dough into workable 1-foot-long pieces.

Now, using the cutting attachment, run the sheets through the cutting slot.

Dust the noodles and a baking sheet with flour or cornmeal (if using). Coil the strands into a nest or hang to dry on a pasta rack, or even on the back of a chair. The important thing is the strands should be separated so they are not touching and sticking together.

Allow the noodles to dry for 10 minutes, or until a little firm and less sticky. This helps prevent the pasta from clumping and sticking together when cooked. Fresh pasta will last several weeks in the refrigerator or can be frozen for up to one month.

Cook pasta as directed (see Master the Basics: Cooking Pasta, on page 96). Toss with just enough sauce to coat, without leaving a big puddle on the bottom of the plate. It's always best to add the pasta to the sauce and not the other way around.

Orecchiette with Broccoli Rabe and Italian Sausage

Recipe courtesy of Joe Bastianich

For the Pasta Pressure Test, Joe Bastianich showcases his family's recipe for this delicate ear-shaped pasta with bitter broccoli rabe and sweet Italian sausage. He says, "An outstanding dish shouldn't be overly complex. Often the best ones are made with only a handful of ingredients. For example, this pasta recipe contains little more than broccoli rabe and sausage. The delicious simplicity of authentic Italian food is what we are looking for. When you think you have enough ingredients, take two out!"

SERVES 4

1 pound broccoli rabe, stems trimmed (see Chef Ingredient: Broccoli Rabe on the opposite page)

1 pound dry orecchiette (little ear-shaped pasta)

¼ cup extra-virgin olive oil

4 sweet Italian sausages, cut on the bias into ½-inch slices (about 1 pound)

4 cloves garlic, minced

½ teaspoon crushed red-pepper flakes

Kosher salt and freshly ground black pepper

Freshly grated Parmesan cheese

Bring a large pot of salted water to a boil. Fill a large bowl with ice water. Add the broccoli rabe to the pot and cook for 4 minutes, or until the spears are slightly tender and bright green. Don't overcook. Use tongs to transfer the rabe to the bowl of ice water. When chilled all the way through, remove the rabe from the water bath and chop into 1-inch chunks. Set aside.

Return the pot of salted water to a boil. Add the orecchiette and stir. Cook for 5 to 8 minutes, or until al dente (see Master the Basics: Cooking Pasta, on page 96). Drain, reserving ½ cup of the pasta cooking water.

Coat a large skillet with the oil and place over medium-high heat. When the oil is hot, add the sausage. Cook and stir for 5 to 7 minutes, or until the sausage is browned and cooked through. Using a slotted spoon, transfer the sausage to a bowl and set aside.

Add the garlic and red-pepper flakes to the pan, stirring for 30 seconds, or until the garlic is fragrant. Add the reserved broccoli rabe, season with salt and pepper, and stir for 1 minute.

Add the sausage back to the pan, along with the orecchiette. Toss to evenly distribute the ingredients, adding reserved cooking liquid if the pasta seems too dry. Sprinkle with cheese and serve immediately.

Broccoli Rabe

Also known as *rapini*, broccoli rabe is one of those vegetables that people tend to either love or hate. Its peppery punch makes it the perfect partner for a variety of pasta dishes. Here its subtle bitterness is a great contrast to the sweetness and richness of the pork. In addition to its distinct flavor, broccoli rabe has a different appearance from regular broccoli and is characterized by ruffled leaves, baby florets, and long stalks. Broccoli rabe can be found year-round at most supermarkets.

COOKING PASTA

In a large pot, heat at least 1 quart of salted water for every 4 ounces of dry pasta. (The salt will season the pasta internally as it absorbs liquid and swells. Your sauce may require less salt when you use salted water for the pasta.) Bring the water to a rolling boil. Add the pasta all at once to the boiling water, and keep the heat high to bring the water back to a boil as quickly as possible (put a lid on the pot, if neces-sary). Cook the pasta, uncovered, at a fast boil, stirring with a wooden spoon during the first minute or two of cooking to prevent sticking. If you don't stir, pieces of pasta that are touching one another will stick together. Frequent stirring ensures that the pasta will cook evenly.

Cook until firm. Pasta should be tender but still firm when you eat it—what the Italians call *al dente*. It means that it offers a slight resistance when bitten into, without being too hard or crunchy. To prevent overcooking, remove a strand from the boiling water with a fork and sample.

When the pasta is done, drain into a large colander standing in the sink, then pick up the colander with its contents and give it a shake to remove excess water. Do not rinse. Rinsing will cool the pasta and prevent absorption of the sauce; the starch that makes the pasta stick to itself also helps the sauce stick to the pasta.

Immediately remove drained pasta from the colander, and either toss it with the sauce or place it in a preheated serving dish or individual preheated serving bowls. Use a fork and spoon and quickly toss it with the sauce.

It's a good idea to reserve a bit of the pasta cooking water to stir into sauce, as the small amount of starch left in the cooking water can thicken your sauce slightly and add moisture to your dish.

Note: Homemade pasta cooks in less time than dry pasta and is more delicate. To cook fresh pasta, gently place the pasta in boiling water, stir to separate, and begin tasting for doneness after 2 minutes. Fresh pasta may also need to be "fluffed" if it has started to stick together.

Fresh Fettuccine with Mushroom Cream Sauce and Roasted Bell Peppers

Recipe courtesy of Mike Kim

"The inspiration for this dish was based on the image of Joe's mom (Chef Lidia Bastianich) making a pasta dish with an assortment of mushrooms," says Mike. "When I saw the shiitake and porcini mushrooms in the pantry, they jumped out to me, and I felt that they would make an earthy and interesting cream sauce, which typically pairs well with fresh egg pasta. The judges, at first, doubted my ingredient selection of mushrooms and roasted peppers, but once they tasted it, they felt that the combination worked well together. Thankfully, this pasta dish kept me safe from elimination!"

SERVES 4

1 ounce dried porcini mushrooms

2 tablespoons olive oil

1 shallot, minced

2 cloves garlic, minced

½ pound shiitake mushrooms, wiped of grit and finely chopped

4 sprigs fresh oregano, leaves striped from the stem, plus more for garnish

Kosher salt and freshly ground black pepper

½ cup dry white wine, such as Pinot Grigio

½ cup Chicken Broth (page 242), or store-bought

1 cup heavy cream

1 pound fresh fettuccine (see Homemade Pasta, on page 92), or store-bought

1 each red and yellow bell peppers, roasted and sliced into strips (see Master the Basics: Roasting Bell Peppers, on page 99)

½ cup freshly grated Parmesan, plus more for garnish

Place the porcini mushrooms in a small bowl. Pour in 1 cup of hot water. Let stand for 20 minutes, or until the mushrooms soften. Line a small mesh strainer with cheesecloth or paper towel and drain the mushrooms, reserving the liquid. Chop the mushrooms and set aside.

In a large skillet, heat the oil over medium-high heat. When the oil is hot, add the shallot and garlic and cook, stirring, for 1 minute, or until just translucent. Add the shiitake and porcini mushrooms and oregano and season with salt and pepper. Cook and stir for 7 minutes, or until the mushrooms begin to brown and release their liquid. Pour in the wine and continue to cook for 2 to 3 minutes, or until evaporated. Pour in the broth and the reserved porcini liquid. Cook for 10 minutes, or until the liquid is reduced. Add the cream, reduce the heat to medium-low, and simmer for 7 to 10 minutes, or until the sauce thickens enough to coat the back of a spoon. Stir occasionally and season with salt and pepper.

(continued)

In a large pot of boiling salted water, cook the fettuccine until al dente (see Master the Basics: Cooking Pasta, on page 96). Drain well. Add the pasta to the skillet, stirring to coat with the sauce. Cook, tossing, for 1 minute, or until the pasta is heated through and well-coated. Remove the pasta from the heat and add ½ cup of Parmesan, tossing to coat. Divide the pasta among 4 warm serving bowls or plates. Garnish each serving with roasted pepper strips, a generous sprinkle of Parmesan, and a shower of fresh oregano leaves. Serve immediately.

ROASTING BELL PEPPERS

Roasting peppers is simple and adds a dramatic sweet-smoky depth of flavor to a variety of dishes. Roasted peppers are one of those staples you should always have in the fridge to enhance any recipe or serve atop crostini for a quick appetizer. Several methods can be used for roasting fresh bell peppers: grilling, charring directly over a gas stove top, broiling, or oven-roasting. Chef Graham Elliot says he prefers oven roasting because "it's the best way to get a silky-soft pepper that slumps on a plate. On a grill and stove top, you are just charring the skin. While those methods might be quicker, you forfeit the deep sweetness and aroma that oven-roasting imparts."

Preheat the oven to 400°F. Brush the peppers with olive oil and arrange them side by side on a baking pan in a single layer.

Roast the peppers for about 15 minutes, until the skins blister. Keep a watchful eye on the peppers to ensure that they do not become too scorched. When dark splotches begin to appear on the peppers, carefully turn them over with tongs.

When the peppers are charred on all sides, remove them from the baking pan using tongs and place them in a bowl. Cover the bowl tightly with plastic wrap, and let the hot peppers steam for about 10 minutes to loosen the skins.

Remove peppers from the bowl and pull off the charred skins. Discard the core, seeds, and skins.

Set peppers aside for use. Do not rinse the peppers! That will wash away the delicious smoky flavor.

Linguini Aglio e Olio (Garlic and Oil)

 Recipe courtesy of MasterChef **Kitchen**

MasterChef judge Graham Elliot describes a good cook as "one who can make a great dish with only a few ingredients and prepare them with care." This pasta recipe is as simple as it gets. In this timeless Italian peasant dish, hot pasta is tossed with lots of fresh garlic sautéed in fruity olive oil, seasoned with a little crushed red pepper, and finished off with a snowy blanket of sharp Parmesan cheese. Serve this dish with a mixed green salad, crusty bread, and your favorite light red wine.

This basic pasta dish leaves much room for improvisation and versatility. Add sautéed zucchini, spinach, steamed broccoli, artichoke hearts, or your favorite grilled vegetables.

SERVES 4

1 pound dry linguini

¼ cup extra-virgin olive oil

6 cloves garlic, minced

2 tablespoons plus 1 teaspoon kosher salt, plus more for seasoning

1 teaspoon red-pepper flakes

¼ cup finely chopped fresh flat-leaf parsley

Freshly ground black pepper

Freshly grated Parmigiano-Reggiano

Bring a large pot of water to a boil over high heat and add 2 tablespoons salt. Add the linguini and stir well. Cook, stirring occasionally, for 8 minutes, or until al dente, tender but not mushy (see Master the Basics: Cooking Pasta, on page 96). Try to time it so that the garlic (below) is done when the pasta is ready.

While the pasta cooks, place a large skillet over low heat and add the oil, garlic, 1 teaspoon salt, and red-pepper flakes. Cook and stir for 3 minutes, or until the garlic softens and then becomes a light golden color. It is important not to let the garlic get too brown as this will result in a bitter, unpleasant taste.

Drain the pasta in a colander set in the sink, reserving about ¼ cup of the starchy cooking water. Add the pasta and the reserved pasta water, a little at a time, to the garlic mixture. Toss well to aerate the pasta, making the sauce slick and creamy. Sprinkle in the parsley, toss well to coat evenly, and season with salt and pepper.

Transfer the pasta to a large warm serving bowl or divide among 4 warm shallow bowls. Pass the grated cheese around the table for serving.

Spaghetti and Meatballs

 Recipe courtesy of MasterChef **Kitchen**

A heaping, hearty platter of spaghetti and meatballs evokes a feeling of comfort and satisfaction—the picture of the perfect family dinner that's sure to please everyone. The stars of this dish are, of course, the meatballs. The trick to making moist, tender meatballs is using bread cubes soaked in milk. The moisture breaks up the beef and pork so the meatballs aren't dense and are softer and more succulent. Just like Grandma used to make!

On the off chance that you end up with leftovers, ladle a few meatballs into a hunk of Italian bread or a crusty roll for a killer meatball sub.

SERVES 4, MAKES 20 MEATBALLS

2 tablespoons olive oil

1 small onion, chopped

2 cloves garlic, minced

Kosher salt and freshly ground black pepper

1 cup cubed day-old Italian bread, crust removed (2 slices)

1 cup whole milk

1 pound ground beef

1 pound ground pork

2 large egg whites, whipped until frothy

2 tablespoons coarsely chopped fresh flat-leaf parsley leaves, plus more for garnish

2 tablespoons coarsely chopped fresh basil leaves

2 tablespoons coarsely chopped fresh oregano leaves

½ cup freshly grated Parmesan, plus more for serving

1 quart Marinara Sauce (page 245) or quality jarred tomato sauce, heated

1 pound dry spaghetti

Preheat the oven to 400°F.

Coat a skillet with the oil and place over medium heat. When the oil is hot, add the onion and garlic and season with salt and pepper. Cook and stir for 5 minutes, or until the vegetables are soft but not colored. Remove the pan from the heat and set aside to cool completely.

Put the bread in a bowl and pour the milk over the bread to moisten. Let it soak for a couple of minutes.

Combine the beef and pork in a large bowl. Add the egg whites, parsley, basil, oregano, Parmesan, and the cooled onion mixture. Season with 2 teaspoons salt and 1 teaspoon pepper. Drain the bread from the milk without squeezing out all of the liquid. Hand-crumble the bread into pea-size pieces and add to the meat mixture. Gently combine all the ingredients with clean hands until just mixed together. Don't overwork the mixture or the meatballs will become tough. Shape the meat mixture into 2-inch balls. You should have about 20 meatballs.

Put the meatballs side by side on a baking pan. Bake for 10 minutes until firm but not completely cooked through.

In the meantime, bring a big pot of salted water to a boil for the spaghetti. In another pot, bring the marinara sauce to a simmer over medium-low heat.

Add the baked meatballs to the sauce and cook, stirring gently with a wooden spoon, for 15 minutes, or until no trace of pink remains at the center of the meatballs.

Add the spaghetti to the boiling water. Return to a boil and cook the pasta for 8 minutes, or until al dente (see Master the Basics: Cooking Pasta, on page 96). Drain the pasta and return it to the pot off of the heat. Ladle in about 2 cups of the sauce, tossing well until the pasta is coated with the sauce. Season with salt and pepper, if necessary.

Serve the pasta in warm bowls or piled high on a large warm platter. Spoon a little more of the sauce over the pasta and shower with chopped parsley. Put the meatballs in a bowl on the side, and pass more Parmesan around the table.

POULTRY

Vietnamese Chicken and Rice with Cabbage Salad

Recipe courtesy of Slim Huynh

Slim arrived at the MasterChef kitchen ready to compete. "I'm serious about this . . . I want to be a chef!" she says. Her sweet and spicy signature dish reflected her personality and was a hit with the judges. Graham Elliot praised the dish as "delicious" and commented, "This homey plate of crisp salad and succulent chicken is surprisingly light yet deeply satisfying. The vegetables soak up all of the liquid, and the salad is spicy but yummy."

SERVES 4

4 (6-ounce) bone-in chicken thighs, rinsed and patted dry

2 bay leaves

Kosher salt

½ teaspoon whole black peppercorns

Juice of 1 lime

1 tablespoon chile sauce, such as Sriracha (see Chef Ingredient: Sriracha Chile Sauce, on page 108)

3 teaspoons fish sauce (see Chef Ingredient: Fish Sauce, on page 108)

2 teaspoons sugar

Freshly ground black pepper

2 large carrots, peeled

1 head (2 pounds) green cabbage, halved, cored, and thinly shredded (about 4 cups)

8 fresh Thai basil leaves, hand-torn (see Chef Ingredient: Thai Basil, on page 108)

3 tablespoons vegetable oil

1 shallot, minced

2 cloves garlic, minced

3 cups broccoli florets

2 scallions, white and green parts, chopped

Steamed jasmine rice

2 tablespoons coarsely chopped unsalted peanuts, for garnish

2 tablespoons whole cilantro leaves, for garnish

Place 1 of the chicken thighs in a small pot and cover with water. Add the bay leaves, 1 teaspoon of salt, and the peppercorns. Heat just to boiling, lower to a gentle simmer, and cook for 5 to 10 minutes. Remove the pot from the heat and cover with a tight-fitting lid. Let the chicken poach in the hot water for 15 minutes, or until cooked through and moist. Remove the chicken to a cutting board to cool. Reserve 1 cup of the poaching liquid.

For the salad, first make the dressing. In a large mixing bowl, combine the lime juice, chile sauce, 1 teaspoon of the fish sauce, and 1 teaspoon of the sugar. Use a small whisk or fork to blend and dissolve the sugar.

Using a vegetable peeler, shave thinly down the length of the carrots so that they fall in ribbons into the bowl with the dressing. Add the cabbage and basil. Once the chicken thigh has cooled enough to handle, shred it into small strips, discarding the skin and bones. Add the chicken to the salad and toss thoroughly to distribute the ingredients evenly. Set aside in the refrigerator to allow the flavors to come together.

(continued)

To prepare the stir-fry, remove and discard the skin from the remaining 3 chicken thighs. Slice the thighs down the center and remove the bone. Coarsely chop the meat into bite-size pieces. Set aside the meat and the bones.

Coat a wok or large skillet with the oil and place over medium-high heat. When the oil is hot, add the shallot, garlic, and the 3 thigh bones (which will add a meaty base flavor). Stir-fry for 30 seconds, or until fragrant. Add the chicken meat and season generously with salt and pepper. Cook for 3 minutes to brown the chicken lightly.

Toss in the broccoli and the remaining 2 teaspoons fish sauce and 1 teaspoon sugar. Pour in about ¼ cup of the reserved chicken poaching liquid, and continue cooking for 10 to 12 minutes, or until the chicken is cooked through and the broccoli is crisp-tender but not limp. Add more poaching liquid as necessary. Remove the pan from the heat and discard the bones. Sprinkle in the scallions and toss to combine.

To serve, put a mound of rice onto the center of each plate and place the chicken and broccoli mixture on top. Garnish with peanuts and cilantro. Serve the cabbage salad on the side.

CHEF INGREDIENTS:

Thai Basil

Thai basil is used often in Vietnamese cuisine as well as in Thai food. Sometimes referred to as "holy basil," the sweetly perfumed herb with small leaves and purple stems has a distinct scent of basil combined with anise or licorice. If you're unable to find Thai basil, you may substitute cilantro for a different, but still authentically Asian flavor.

Sriracha Chile Sauce

Sriracha (SIR-rotch-ah) sauce—also affectionately known as "rooster sauce" because of the strutting rooster emblazoned on the label—is a blend of tomatoes, chiles, garlic, vinegar, and sugar. Used as a condiment or seasoning, the fiery sauce has developed an almost cultlike following and has become a mainstream favorite among foodies, popping up in grocery stores all over the country. It's often used in Asian cooking but lends itself well to a variety of other cuisines. Try it on pizza, a plate of scrambled eggs, or mix with ketchup and spread on a burger.

Fish Sauce

Indispensable in Southeast Asian cuisine, fish sauce, or *nam pla*, imparts a distinct aroma and complex flavor. The base of the fish sauce is, naturally, fish. Good-quality fish sauce is made from a mixture of anchovies and salt that has been fermented in wooden barrels for one year. Look for it in the Asian food section of your grocery store or at specialty food markets.

Nutty Orange Chicken with Rice

Recipe courtesy of Mike Kim

As the winner of the Invention Test, Mike received an important advantage: the ability to choose his team members for the next challenge. Mike's stir-fry blew away the rest of the pack. In Gordon's words, the dish was "head and shoulders above the competition."

About his method of searing the chicken breasts wrapped in foil, Mike says, "A chef once told me about this technique: Before searing the chicken breast, make a collar of foil and create an oval ring. This allows the skin to cook longer and become really crispy, without overcooking the breast meat."

SERVES 4

1 cup jasmine rice

2½ cups Chicken Broth (page 242), or quality store-bought

3 mandarin oranges, unpeeled

2 whole star anise

4 (6-ounce) boneless chicken breasts

2 teaspoons Chinese five-spice powder (see Chef Ingredient: Chinese Five-Spice Powder, on page 111)

Kosher salt and freshly ground black pepper

6 tablespoons peanut oil

3 tablespoons cornstarch

1-inch piece fresh ginger, peeled and minced (about 2 tablespoons)

3 cloves garlic, minced

2 scallions, white and light green parts, sliced

1 each red and yellow bell pepper, halved, cored, seeded, and thinly sliced

2 dried red chiles

2 tablespoons peanuts

2 tablespoons cashews

¾ pound green beans

2 tablespoons soy sauce

1 tablespoon rice vinegar

Combine the rice and 2 cups of the broth in a pot over medium heat. Using a vegetable peeler, peel 1 of the oranges, taking care to just get the skin and none of the bitter white pith, then add the zest strips to the rice. Set the orange aside. Add 1 star anise to the rice and bring to a boil. Reduce the heat to low, cover, and simmer for 20 minutes.

Preheat the oven to 350°F.

Tear off four 12-inch pieces of aluminum foil and form each into an oval ring about the size of the chicken breasts. Season both sides of the chicken breasts generously with the five-spice powder, salt, and pepper. Set the chicken inside the ring, skin side down, and form the foil so it fits snuggly around the chicken like a collar.

(continued)

Coat an ovenproof skillet with 2 tablespoons of the oil and place over medium-high heat. When the oil is hot, lay the chicken in the pan, skin side down. Only the skin should be touching the pan, not the meat itself. Sear the chicken skin for 5 minutes, or until crisp and light brown. Remove the chicken from the pan and remove the foil ring. Put the chicken back in the pan, skin side up. Transfer the chicken to the oven to finish cooking for 15 to 20 minutes. In the meantime make the stir-fry.

Slice the remaining 2 unpeeled oranges into paper-thin slices. Toss the slices with 2 tablespoons of the cornstarch. Pour the remaining 4 tablespoons peanut oil into a large skillet or wok and place over high heat. When the oil is smoking hot, quickly fry the orange slices for 3 to 5 minutes. Frying removes the bitterness from the skin, and the slices become crispy so you can eat them whole. The oil will spatter a bit. Carefully remove the orange slices and drain on a plate lined with paper towels. Their shape should remain intact.

Keep the pan on the heat. Stir-fry the ginger, garlic, scallions, peppers, chiles, peanuts, cashews, and the remaining star anise. Add the green beans and season with salt and pepper. Mix the remaining ½ cup broth with the remaining 1 tablespoon cornstarch and add it to the pan. Squeeze in the juice of the reserved orange (about 1 tablespoon) along with the soy sauce and vinegar. Cook, stirring, for 5 to 7 minutes, or until the sauce is thick and the vegetables are tender.

To serve, slice the chicken breasts on the bias. Mound the rice on 4 plates and put a few spoonfuls of the vegetable stir-fry on top, making sure to get a bit of everything. Layer the chicken slices in an overlapping pattern on top, skin side up, and garnish with the fried orange slices. Drizzle with any remaining sauce.

CHEF INGREDIENT:

Chinese Five-Spice Powder

This aromatic blend of spices combines the five primary flavors of Chinese cuisine: sweet, sour, pungent, bitter, and salty. Typically made from star anise, cinnamon, cloves, fennel, and peppercorns, five-spice powder can be used in virtually everything from fish, pork, and poultry to vegetable and rice dishes. It can be found in the spice aisle of most grocery stores and at Asian food markets.

Chicken Tikka Masala

Recipe courtesy of Sheetal Bhagat

Sheetal, who was raised in a traditional Indian household, brought the cuisine of her heritage to the judges for her signature dish. The judges said that Sheetal's rich, creamy, lightly spiced chicken dish evoked the sensory delights of the small streets of an Indian village.

SERVES 4

2 (2-pound) whole boneless, skinless chicken breasts, cut into large chunks

1 cup plain yogurt

6 tablespoons Tikka Masala paste, such as Patak's

1 tablespoon fresh lemon juice

6 tablespoons extra-virgin olive oil

Kosher salt and freshly ground black pepper

2 red bell peppers, quartered, cored, and seeded

4 large tomatoes, quartered

1 large onion, quartered

1 cup Chicken Broth (page 242), or quality store-bought

6 cloves garlic, crushed

1 tablespoon ground cumin

1 tablespoon ground coriander

½ tablespoon chili powder

½ cup heavy cream

2 tablespoons chopped fresh cilantro leaves

Steamed basmati rice

Put the chicken in a large resealable plastic bag. In a small bowl, mix together the yogurt, 2 tablespoons of the Tikka Masala paste, the lemon juice, and 2 tablespoons of the oil. Season with salt and pepper. Pour the marinade into the bag, squeeze the air out, and seal. Move the bag around to evenly coat the chicken with the yogurt mixture. Set aside at room temperature.

Preheat the broiler.

Put the peppers, tomatoes, and onion cut side down on a baking pan. Drizzle with 2 tablespoons of the oil and season with salt and pepper. Broil the vegetables for 10 to 12 minutes, or until they are nicely charred. Let the vegetables cool for 5 minutes. Carefully transfer the vegetables to a food processor and purée until smooth. Set aside.

In a mixing bowl, combine the broth with the remaining 4 tablespoons Tikka Masala paste, whisking to dissolve and fully incorporate. Set aside.

Coat a large skillet or Dutch oven with the remaining 2 tablespoons oil and place over medium-low heat. When the oil is hot, add the garlic, cumin, coriander, and chili powder. Cook for 1 minute, stirring well so the spices do not scorch. Pour in the Masala broth and vegetable purée and bring to a simmer, stirring to combine. Remove the chicken from the marinade and add to the pan. Cook and stir for 15 minutes, or until the chicken is cooked through. Stir in the cream and cook for 10 minutes longer, or until the sauce is thick. Sprinkle with cilantro and serve with steamed rice.

Smothered Chicken with Bacon Brussels Sprouts

Recipe courtesy of Tracy Nailor

Tracy, a physician from Atlanta, cooked up homestyle comfort food for her signature dish, which was based on her mother's original handwritten recipe. With tears in her eyes, Tracy explained to the judges how much her mother had loved to cook. "About a year before my mom died, I asked her to write down the family recipes. After she passed, I started cooking all of her dishes because I wanted to hold on to her and taste her flavors." After sampling this hearty chicken dish, the judges agreed that Tracy had indeed honored her mother's memory with this delicious dish.

SERVES 4

1 cup all-purpose flour

½ teaspoon sweet paprika

½ teaspoon cayenne pepper

½ teaspoon granulated garlic

Kosher salt and freshly ground black pepper

4 (4-ounce) boneless, skinless chicken breasts, rinsed and patted dry

4 tablespoons olive oil

1 medium onion, chopped

2 cups Chicken Broth (page 242), or quality store-bought

2 sprigs fresh rosemary, needles stripped from the stem and chopped

½ pound Brussels sprouts

4 bacon slices, cut into 1-inch pieces

1 shallot, halved lengthwise and sliced

Steamed long grain white rice

Combine the flour, paprika, cayenne, garlic, 1 teaspoon of the salt, and ½ teaspoon of the pepper in a pie plate, mixing together with your fingers. Season the chicken breasts on both sides with salt and pepper. Dredge the seasoned chicken in the flour mixture, shaking off the excess.

Coat a large skillet, preferably cast-iron, with 2 tablespoons of oil and place over medium heat. When the oil is hot, lay the chicken in the pan. Brown for 3 to 5 minutes on each side, until the outside is nicely browned. Remove the chicken to a side platter.

To the drippings in the pan, add 1 tablespoon of the oil and the onion. Season with salt and pepper. Cook and stir for 3 minutes, or until the onions are soft and starting to brown. Pour the broth into the pan and bring to a boil, stirring. Return the chicken to the pan, toss in the rosemary, and gently simmer for 5 minutes, or until the sauce thickens.

Prepare the Brussels sprouts by cutting off the brown ends and pulling off any yellow outer leaves. Cut the sprouts in half lengthwise.

Coat a large skillet with the remaining 1 tablespoon oil and place over medium heat. Add the bacon and cook, stirring, for 2 minutes to render some of the fat. Add the shallot, stirring to coat, and cook for 5 to 7 minutes, or until the bacon is crisp and the shallot is caramelized. Using a slotted spoon, remove the bacon and shallot to a little side bowl.

To the drippings in the pan, add the sprouts and season with salt and pepper. Spread the sprouts out so all of them are touching the hot pan. Once they start to brown, toss and cooking for 10 minutes longer, or until the sprouts are tender. Season again with salt and pepper before serving.

To serve, pile a bit of rice on each plate and put a piece of chicken on top. Ladle the sauce on top of the chicken to smother. Scatter the Brussels sprouts around the plate and sprinkle the bacon-shallot mixture on top.

Asian Orange Stir-Fry

Recipe courtesy of Jenna Hamiter

Jenna says as soon as Gordon Ramsay announced the guidelines of this Invention Challenge—to make a Chinese-inspired dish featuring mandarin oranges—she knew she wanted to create a healthier alternative to the traditional deep-fried orange chicken dish served at many Chinese restaurants. Crisp, fresh, and colorful, with crunchy snow peas, sweet mandarins, and tender chicken, Jenna's healthy orange chicken makeover is flavorful and ready in less than an hour.

SERVES 4

1 large egg white

1 tablespoon cornstarch

1 teaspoon sesame oil

½ teaspoon cayenne pepper

Kosher salt and freshly ground black pepper

1½ pounds boneless, skinless chicken breasts, cut into 2-inch chunks

3 mandarin oranges, segmented, juice reserved (see Master the Basics: Segmenting Citrus, on page 53)

½ cup Chicken Broth (page 242), or quality store-bought

2 tablespoons rice vinegar

2 tablespoons dark brown sugar, loosely packed

3 tablespoons soy sauce

1 tablespoon finely grated fresh ginger

1 tablespoon finely grated garlic

½ teaspoon red-pepper flakes

1 teaspoon chili sauce, such as Sriracha (see Chef Ingredient: Sriracha Chile Sauce, on page 108)

3 tablespoons vegetable oil

½ pound snow peas

4 cups cooked white rice (see Cooking Rice, on page 247)

2 scallions, white and green parts, thinly sliced on the bias, for garnish

In a mixing bowl, whisk together the egg white, cornstarch, sesame oil, and cayenne. Season with ½ teaspoon salt and ¼ teaspoon pepper. Add the chicken and toss to coat in the marinade. Set aside.

To the reserved orange juice, add the broth, vinegar, sugar, soy sauce, ginger, garlic, red-pepper flakes, and chili sauce. Stir to dissolve the sugar.

Coat a large skillet or wok with the vegetable oil and place over medium-high heat. When the oil is hot, add the chicken chunks in batches and fry for 3 minutes, or until almost completely cooked through. Remove the chicken to a plate lined with paper towel to drain. Repeat with the remaining chicken. To the drippings in the pan, add the snow peas. Toss to coat, then pour in the orange juice mixture. Simmer for 5 minutes, or until the sauce is thick and the peas are tender. Add the chicken back into the pan, tossing to coat in the sauce.

To serve, put a cup of rice in a bowl or ramekin and pack it in gently. Invert the bowl onto a dinner plate. Put a few spoonfuls of the orange chicken stir-fry next to the rice. Garnish with scallions and orange segments.

Stuffed Chicken Parmesan with Roasted Cherry Tomato Sauce

Recipe courtesy of Whitney Miller

For this Head-to-Head Challenge, Whitney put a modern spin on an Italian classic: Chicken Parmesan. Using cherry tomatoes lends sweetness to the sauce, and roasting them adds an extra dimension of flavor. Bold anchovies and garlic wake up the chicken, and the combination of flavorful chicken, rich sauce, creamy mozzarella, and fresh basil make this dish something special.

SERVES 4

FOR THE TOMATO SAUCE

1 pint cherry tomatoes, halved

4 tablespoons olive oil

Kosher salt and freshly ground black pepper

1 shallot, minced

2 cloves garlic, minced

6 large basil leaves, leaves stacked, rolled into a cigar, and sliced into ribbons

FOR THE FILLING

2 anchovies, rinsed and coarsely chopped

2 cloves garlic, coarsely chopped

6 ounces fresh mozzarella, cut into ½-inch cubes

4 large basil leaves, leaves stacked, rolled into a cigar, and sliced into ribbons, plus extra leaves for garnish

Kosher salt and freshly ground black pepper

FOR THE CHICKEN PARMESAN

4 (4-ounce) boneless, skinless chicken breasts

Kosher salt and freshly ground black pepper

½ cup all-purpose flour

2 large eggs beaten with 1 tablespoon water

1½ cups plain dry bread crumbs

½ cup freshly grated Parmesan

1 tablespoon olive oil

2 tablespoons unsalted butter

Preheat the oven to 350°F.

To make the tomato sauce: Spread the tomatoes out on a baking pan, cut side down. Drizzle with 2 tablespoons of the oil and season with ½ teaspoon each of salt and pepper. Bake for 15 minutes, or until the tomatoes have shriveled a bit and the skins begin to pull away. Remove the roasted tomatoes from the oven and set aside.

Coat a skillet with the remaining 2 tablespoons oil and place over medium-low heat. When the oil is hot, add the shallot and garlic. Cook and stir for 2 minutes, or until caramelized. Add the basil and the reserved tomatoes, along with any collected juices. Season with ¼ teaspoon each salt and pepper. Reduce the heat to low and simmer for 10 to 15 minutes, stirring.

(continued)

To make the filling: Combine the anchovies and garlic using a mortar and pestle. Smash to create a paste. Place in a small bowl and combine it with the mozzarella, basil, salt, and pepper. Set the filling aside at room temperature.

To make the chicken Parmesan: Season both sides of the chicken breasts generously with salt and pepper.

Set up an assembly line: a dish of flour seasoned with salt and pepper, a shallow dish with the beaten egg and water, and a plate with bread crumbs combined with the Parmesan.

Working with one piece of chicken at a time, dredge it first in the flour, shaking off the excess.

Next, place the floured chicken into the egg wash, coating it completely and letting the excess drip back into the bowl. Then dredge the chicken in the bread crumb mixture, gently pressing in the crumbs. Set the chicken aside on a large plate and continue with the remaining chicken.

Using a knife, make a 2-inch-long incision down the center of each chicken breast, taking care not to break through the bottom half. Fill the pocket with the mozzarella mixture, packing it in tightly.

Place a large ovenproof skillet over medium heat and add the oil and butter. When the butter has melted, put the chicken in the pan stuffed side up. Brown for 1 to 2 minutes. Carefully turn the chicken breasts over and brown the other side for 2 minutes, or until golden. Transfer the skillet to the oven and cook for 10 minutes, or until the cheese is melted and the chicken is no longer pink.

To assemble, cut the chicken breasts diagonally into 1-inch slices. Layer the slices in an overlapping pattern on the base of the plate, allowing the cheese to ooze out. Spoon some of the tomato sauce on top. Garnish with fresh basil.

Chicken Pot Pie

 Recipe courtesy of MasterChef **Kitchen**

This rendition of the old-fashioned, heartwarming original is so good, you won't even miss the cream. Frozen puff pastry sheets work well here without compromising the dish. If you're pressed for time, skip the first step of boiling the chicken and buy a whole rotisserie chicken and a quart of good, low-sodium canned chicken broth at the grocery store. It may not be totally homemade, but the result is easy as pie.

Serving individual pot pies makes for a great presentation. You can purchase crocks or 2-cup ramekins at any kitchen store if you don't already have them.

SERVES 4

1 (2½-pound) whole chicken

1 teaspoon salt

3 carrots, diced, trimmings reserved

2 celery stalks, diced, trimmings reserved

1 small onion, diced, trimmings reserved

¼ cup (½ stick) unsalted butter

Kosher salt and freshly ground black pepper

½ cup all-purpose flour

1 large potato, peeled, diced, and cooked (about 2 cups)

¾ cup frozen sweet peas, thawed

2 tablespoons finely chopped fresh flat-leaf parsley

1 frozen puff pastry sheet, thawed

1 large egg, lightly beaten

Put the chicken in a large stockpot and cover with ½ gallon of cool water. Add the salt and the carrot, celery, and onion trimmings. Bring up to a boil over medium-high heat. Simmer, uncovered, for 45 minutes, or until the chicken is just cooked through, skimming frequently as the oil rises to the surface. Remove the chicken to a cutting board to cool. Continue to cook down the chicken broth for 10 minutes longer to condense the flavor, until it's reduced to 4 cups.

Strain the chicken broth into a large bowl or measuring cup and discard the vegetable solids. Set the broth aside. When cool enough to handle, shred the chicken meat into bite-size pieces. Discard the skin and bones. Transfer the chicken to a large bowl.

Preheat the oven to 400°F.

In a large pot or Dutch oven, melt the butter over medium heat. Add the carrots, celery, and onion and season with salt and pepper. Cook and stir for 5 minutes, or until the vegetables are tender. Sprinkle the vegetables with the flour. Cook and stir until the flour dissolves.

Gradually whisk in the reserved chicken broth, stirring to prevent lumps. Simmer and whisk for 10 minutes, or until the sauce starts to thicken. It should look like cream of chicken soup.

Mix in the potatoes, peas, parsley, and shredded chicken. Season again with salt and pepper. Simmer for 1 or 2 minutes, stirring, until all the ingredients are well-combined. Remove from the heat.

Lay the puff pastry sheet on a lightly floured surface and roll out slightly. Cut the pastry into four squares.

Fill the crocks or ramekins with the chicken mixture. Cap each with a pastry square, pressing the dough around the rim to form a seal. Lightly beat the egg with 1 tablespoon of water to make an egg wash and brush on the pastry. Set individual pies on a baking pan and transfer to the oven. Bake for 20 minutes, or until the pastry is puffed and golden.

Holiday Roast Turkey
with Herb Butter and Giblet Gravy

 Recipe courtesy of MasterChef **Kitchen**

Succulent, tender, and aromatic, roast turkey is an American classic that all cooks should know how to make. There are a lot of schools of thought on how to master the perfect roast turkey. Graham Elliot's philosophy is the simpler, the better. "I don't truss or change the oven temperature 50 times. I like to start roasting the turkey breast side down to protect it from the initial intense heat. Gravity works, so all of the juices gather in the breast meat during the first half of cooking and keep the meat really moist. Then I turn the bird over to finish cooking and brown the breast."

This recipe doesn't include stuffing—most families have their own closely guarded recipe for that!

SERVES 8

½ cup (1 stick) unsalted butter, at room temperature

2 tablespoons chopped fresh flat-leaf parsley leaves, plus 10 whole sprigs

2 teaspoons chopped fresh thyme leaves, plus 10 whole sprigs

2 teaspoons chopped fresh rosemary needles, plus 8 whole sprigs

2 teaspoons chopped fresh sage leaves, plus 8 whole sprigs

Kosher salt and freshly ground black pepper

1 lemon

1 (12–14-pound) whole fresh turkey, preferably organic, liver discarded, neck and giblets reserved

Olive oil

4 onions, quartered

4 carrots, cut into large chunks

4 celery stalks, cut into large chunks

2 cups Chicken Broth (page 242), or quality store-bought

2 tablespoons all-purpose flour

Adjust a rack at the lowest position in the oven and remove the other racks. Preheat the oven to 350°F.

Combine the softened butter and chopped parsley, thyme, rosemary, and sage in a mixing bowl. Season with ½ teaspoon salt and ¼ teaspoon pepper. Zest the lemon and add to the butter mixture. Mash with a fork or spoon until the herbs are well-incorporated and the butter is flecked with green. Transfer 1 generous tablespoon of the mixture to another small bowl and reserve. Let it stand at room temperature.

Rinse the turkey inside and out under cold running water. Pat dry with paper towels.

Starting at neck end, run your fingers between the skin and meat to loosen the skin from the breast, legs, and thighs, taking care not to tear. Smear the softened herb butter under the skin, massaging and distributing it evenly. Drizzle the skin of the turkey all over with a couple of tablespoons of oil. Season generously with salt and pepper—you should see the seasoning on the skin.

Cut the lemon in half and squeeze the juice inside the cavity and rub all over. This will take away some of the gaminess. Sprinkle the cavity generously with salt and pepper. Stuff the cavity with a couple of pieces of onion and a few sprigs each of parsley, thyme, rosemary, and sage. Loosely tie the drumsticks together with kitchen string to hold the aromatics inside the bird.

Fit a large roasting pan with a V-shaped rack or a wire cooking rack. Place the turkey breast side down on the rack and tuck the wing tips under.

Scatter half of the onions, carrots, and celery around the turkey. Drizzle with 1 tablespoon of oil and season with salt and pepper. Add the 1 tablespoon of reserved herb butter to the roasting pan. Pour in the broth, which will keep the drippings from burning and create a delicious pan sauce.

Roast the turkey for 1 hour, basting periodically with the pan juices or oil. Remove the pan from the oven (closing the oven door to retain heat) and carefully turn the turkey over, breast side up. Cook for another 2½ hours, basting periodically. The turkey should take about 3 hours to cook (around 15 minutes per pound). If the legs or breast brown too quickly, cover them with foil.

While the turkey is cooking, start the giblet gravy. Put the reserved turkey neck and giblets in a large pot and add the remaining onions, carrots, and celery as well as the remaining herb sprigs. Pour in enough water to cover the ingredients by 1 inch.

(continued)

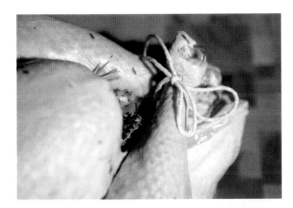

Bring to a boil over high heat, and then reduce the heat to medium-low. Simmer for 2 hours, periodically skimming the foam that rises to the surface. Strain the broth to remove the neck and giblets. Set aside.

The turkey is done when an instant-read thermometer inserted into the meatiest part of the thigh registers 165°F. (The thigh juices will run clear when pricked with a knife.) Transfer the turkey to a cutting board and let it rest for 20 minutes before carving so the juices can settle back into the meat.

Meanwhile, finish the gravy. Remove and discard the vegetable pieces in the roasting pan. Carefully pour the pan drippings through a fine-mesh strainer set over a large measuring cup. Skim off and discard all but 2 table-spoons of the fat that rises to the top. Pour the strained drippings into a pot and place over medium heat.

Whisk the flour into the drippings, stirring as it thickens to prevent lumps. Pour in the giblet broth and bring to a simmer. Season with salt and pepper. Cook for 3 minutes, or until the gravy has reduced slightly.

Carve the turkey (see Master the Basics: Carve a Turkey on the opposite page) and serve with the giblet gravy.

CARVING A TURKEY

Using a sharp knife, cut between the leg and the body to remove the thigh and drumstick together. Do this on both sides. Separate the drumsticks from the thighs by cutting through the joint, then slip the knife into the joint to remove the wings from the body on each side.

Cut clean against the breast bone on one side to remove the breast.

Carve thin slices off of the breast, making parallel cuts. Repeat with the other side.

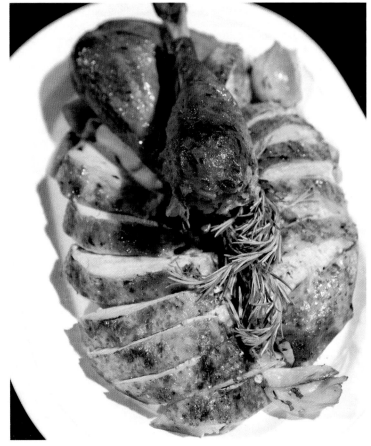

SEAFOOD

Catfish Acadiana with Creamy Shrimp Butter Sauce

Recipe courtesy of Avis White

For her signature dish, Avis White cooked up her down-home Cajun-style catfish. The New Orleans grandma explained, "The judges went crazy over this crispy catfish but felt the pasta was a little heavy, so I took their advice, made some changes, and perfected this recipe." After tasting her Southern feel-good food, Graham Elliot said, "To be a Master-Chef you have to be giving and passionate—and you possess that!"

SERVES 4

2 tablespoons vegetable oil

5 tablespoons unsalted butter

4 scallions, white and green parts, chopped

1 tablespoon all-purpose flour

1 cup heavy cream

Kosher salt and freshly ground black pepper

½ pound large shrimp, tails removed, peeled, and deveined (see Master the Basics: Peeling and Deveining Shrimp, on page 162)

1 cup broccoli florets, blanched (see Master the Basics: Blanching, on page 132)

1 cup cauliflower florets, blanched (see Master the Basics: Blanching)

½ cup cornmeal

4 (6-ounce) catfish fillets

½ cup peanut oil

½ pound dry angel hair pasta, cooked al dente and drained

Chopped fresh flat-leaf parsley

Coat a pot with the vegetable oil, place over medium heat, and add 1 tablespoon of the butter. When the butter is foamy, add the scallions and cook for 1 minute to soften slightly. Sprinkle in the flour, stirring well with a wooden spoon to dissolve. When a thick paste has formed, pour in the cream. Season with ½ teaspoon salt and ¼ teaspoon pepper. Toss in the shrimp and reduce the heat to low. Simmer for 5 minutes, or until the cream sauce reduces slightly. Add the broccoli and cauliflower, stirring to combine. Cook for 2 to 3 minutes, or until the cream sauce thickens and the shrimp are cooked through.

To prepare the catfish, put the cornmeal on a shallow plate and season with ½ teaspoon salt and ½ teaspoon pepper. Dredge the catfish fillets in the seasoned cornmeal, coating both sides evenly. Coat a large skillet with the peanut oil and place over medium heat. When the oil is hot, lay the fillets in the pan, 2 at a time if possible. Fry for 3 to 5 minutes, or until you have a nice crust on the fish. Flip the catfish over and fry for 2 minutes longer. Remove the catfish to a platter lined with paper towels to absorb some of the excess oil.

To serve, toss the pasta with a couple of ladles of the shrimp and vegetable cream sauce. Put a mound of pasta on the plates and lay a catfish fillet across the center. Garnish with chopped parsley.

BLANCHING

Blanching is a technique that many chefs use to preserve flavor, color, and texture. It simply requires briefly submerging an ingredient—most often a vegetable—in boiling water, and then removing it and immediately plunging it into a bowl of ice water, usually referred to as an "ice bath." Blanching is also a great way to prep vegetables in advance. Often times restaurants pre-blanch vegetables before dinner service begins.

Before you begin blanching, create an ice bath by filling a large bowl with cold water and ice cubes. Set aside. Bring a large pot of lightly salted water to a rolling boil. Add the vegetable and return the water to boiling as quickly as possible. Cooking time varies with the vegetable and size of the pieces. As a guideline, the smaller it is, the less time it takes.

Boil the vegetable until it's barely cooked through and just tender. To test, remove one piece with a slotted spoon, dip it into the ice bath to cool, and taste it. When the vegetable is done, quickly remove it from boiling water with a pair of tongs.

Immediately plunge the vegetable into the ice bath to "shock" it and stop the cooking process. Remove the vegetable from the ice bath as soon as it is no longer warm. Spread out to dry on paper towels.

Blackened Catfish Taco with Mango Chutney and Cilantro Black Beans

Recipe courtesy of Whitney Miller

At just 22 years old, Whitney Miller was one of the youngest contestants of the bunch. The small-town Mississippi girl had big dreams of becoming America's MasterChef. On her first day of competition, Whitney told the judges, "I've been cooking since was I was 13 years old, already almost half of my life! I make dinner every night for my family, and I want to be a chef."

To keep the dish light, Whitney grills the catfish instead of frying it. The versatile mango chutney is also delicious served with chicken.

SERVES 4, MAKES 1½ CUPS CHUTNEY

FOR THE CHUTNEY

1 ripe mango, halved and cubed (See Master the Basics: Cubing a Mango, on page 46)

1 red bell pepper, halved, cored, seeded, and chopped

½ onion, chopped

½ small jalapeño chile pepper, finely chopped (wear plastic gloves when handling)

1 clove garlic, minced

1 teaspoon freshly grated ginger

3 tablespoons light brown sugar

Juice of 2 limes

1 teaspoon white vinegar

1 teaspoon balsamic vinegar

Kosher salt and freshly ground black pepper

FOR THE BLACK BEANS

2 tablespoons corn oil

½ onion, chopped

½ small jalapeño chile pepper, finely chopped (wear plastic gloves when handling)

2 cloves garlic, minced

½ teaspoon ground cumin

Kosher salt and freshly ground black pepper

1 can (15 ounces) black beans, rinsed and drained

Juice of 1 lime

¼ cup chopped fresh cilantro leaves, plus more for garnish

FOR THE TACO

2 tablespoons granulated garlic

2 tablespoons chili powder

2 tablespoons onion powder

1 tablespoon sweet paprika

½ tablespoon ground cumin

1 teaspoon cayenne pepper

2 (8-ounce) catfish fillets, rinsed and patted dry, halved crosswise

2 tablespoons corn oil

8 (6-inch) flour tortillas

½ cup finely shredded romaine lettuce

1 ripe avocado, halved, pitted, peeled, and cut into cubes

½ cup sour cream

(continued)

To make the chutney: In a pot over medium heat, combine the mango, bell pepper, onion, jalapeño, garlic, ginger, brown sugar, lime juice, and vinegars. Season with salt and pepper. Cook for 20 minutes, or until the chutney thickens, stirring occasionally. Remove from the heat and cover to keep warm.

To make the black beans: Coat a pot with the oil and place over medium-low heat. When the oil is hot, add the onion, jalapeño, and garlic. Season with cumin, salt, and pepper. Cook and stir for 2 minutes, or until the vegetables are softened and fragrant. Mix in the beans and cook for 5 minutes longer, stirring occasionally. Remove from the heat. Squeeze in the lime juice and stir in the cilantro. Cover to keep warm.

To make the tacos: In a pie plate, combine the granulated garlic, chili powder, onion powder, paprika, cumin, and cayenne. Mix with a fork to evenly distribute the spices. Dredge both sides of the catfish pieces in the spice mixture to evenly coat, tapping off the excess.

Brush a large grill pan with the oil and place over medium-high heat. When the oil begins to smoke, lay the catfish in the pan and grill for 3 to 5 minutes. Turn the fish over and grill for 3 minutes longer, or until the fish is completely cooked through. Remove the fish to a cutting board and shred into pieces using two forks. Put the tortillas on the grill for 30 seconds on each side to warm them up.

To serve, put 2 tortillas on each plate and top with a heaping spoonful of the black beans. Divide the catfish among the tortillas. Put a spoonful of the chutney on top, and garnish with shredded lettuce, avocado, sour cream, and cilantro.

New England-Style Bouillabaisse with French Bread Croutons and Rouille

Recipe courtesy of Dave Miller

When Boston native Dave Miller first entered the judging room, he didn't make the best impression. His bravado left a sour taste in the judges' mouths. Gordon Ramsay questioned the young software engineer for his audacity to consider this basic "fish stew" a refined, complex bouillabaisse but, in the end, the judge believed he had real potential. Joe predicted, "He's going to make a huge transformation."

SERVES 6

1 pound firm white fish fillet, such as cod, haddock, or sea bass, cut into 3-ounce chunks

½ pound large shrimp, peeled and deveined, tails on (see Master the Basics: Peeling and Deveining Shrimp, on page 162)

½ pound sea scallops

½ cup extra-virgin olive oil

Juice of ½ lemon

2 pinches saffron threads

1 tablespoon unsalted butter

1 white onion, thinly sliced

1 leek, white part only, sliced and rinsed well (see Master the Basics: Cleaning Leeks, on page 83)

1 fennel bulb, cored and thinly sliced, fronds reserved for garnish

6 sprigs fresh thyme

6 cloves garlic, minced

Kosher salt and freshly ground black pepper

1 cup dry white wine, such as Sauvignon Blanc

1 pound mussels, scrubbed

1 pound littleneck clams, scrubbed

2 plum (Roma) tomatoes, cored and cut into quarters

1 quart prepared store-bought fish stock

2 large egg yolks

2 pinches cayenne pepper

1 (1-foot-long) French baguette, cut on a diagonal into ½-inch slices (20 slices) and lightly toasted

Put the fish, shrimp, and scallops in a large bowl and coat with ¼ cup of the oil, the lemon juice, and a good pinch of saffron threads. Toss gently with your hands to bleed out the color of the saffron and coat the seafood well. Set aside at room temperature.

Coat a large pot or Dutch oven with 2 tablespoons of the oil and the butter and place over medium heat. When the butter is foamy, add the onion, leek, fennel, thyme, half of the garlic, and another pinch of saffron. Season with salt and pepper. Cook and stir for 5 to 8 minutes, or until the vegetables cook down and soften. Pour in the wine and cook for 3 minutes longer, or until almost completely evaporated.

Put the reserved seafood and the mussels and clams into the pot, along with the tomato wedges. Stir with a wooden spoon to coat the fish with the vegetables. Pour in the stock and bring up to a simmer. Cook for 8 to 12 minutes, or until the fish is opaque.

To make the rouille, put the egg yolks, cayenne, and the remaining garlic in a small mixing bowl. Beat with a whisk or handheld electric mixer. While beating, drizzle the remaining 2 tablespoons oil in a steady stream until the rouille is thick and well-blended, about the consistency of mayonnaise. Season generously with salt and pepper.

To serve, spoon the rouille over the toasted baguette slices and place on a serving platter. Ladle the soup into individual serving bowls, with the toast on the side for dunking. Garnish with reserved fennel fronds.

Halibut with Sweet Corn Zabaglione and Fava Bean Salad

Recipe courtesy of Cat Cora

Celebrity Chef Cat Cora dropped by the MasterChef kitchen to demonstrate her signature dish: Halibut with Sweet Corn Zabaglione. Sharone Hakman, who had to compete against this legendary chef in a head-to-head blind taste test, was honored to be in her company. "I'm excited, nervous, proud, and happy," he said. "It's a dream to cook next to *the* Cat Cora. I'm going to brag about this day for the rest of my life!"

SERVES 4

½ pound fava beans, unshelled (see Master the Basics: Shucking Fava Beans, on page 140)

4 tablespoons extra-virgin olive oil

½ cup diced yellow onions

1 cup fresh yellow corn kernels, cut from 2 ears

1 teaspoon minced garlic

Kosher salt and freshly ground black pepper

2 cups heavy cream

1 large egg yolk

1 teaspoons truffle shavings (optional)

1 cup baby spinach

1 cup halved cherry tomatoes

½ cup thinly sliced red onions

1 lime, halved

4 (6-ounce) halibut fillets

Bring a pot of salted water to a boil. Fill a large bowl with a tray of ice cubes and a couple of cups of water to create an ice bath.

Remove the fava beans from the pods. Put the favas in the boiling salted water and cook for 2 minutes, or until just tender. Use a handheld strainer to remove the favas from the pot and plunge into the ice bath. Once completely cool, pinch the favas out of their husk and put into a mixing bowl. Set aside.

To make the zabaglione, heat 2 tablespoons of oil in a 2- to 3-quart pot over medium heat and add the onions. Cook for 3 minutes, or until the onions are translucent. Add ¾ cup of the corn and the garlic. Season with salt and pepper. Cook for 3 to 4 minutes, or until the corn is tender but not mushy. Pour in the cream, reduce the heat to medium-low, and simmer for 10 minutes, or until slightly thickened, stirring occasionally.

Carefully transfer the creamed corn mixture to a blender, hold the lid down securely with a kitchen towel, and purée until smooth. Pass the corn mixture through a fine-mesh strainer into a heatproof bowl, pressing down with the back of a spoon to extract as much corn juice as possible. Discard the solids.

Bring a pot of water to a simmer and place the bowl with the corn on top, being sure to not let the bottom of the bowl touch the water. Whisk in the egg yolk and truffle shavings (if using). Season with a healthy pinch of salt and pepper. Whisk for 10 minutes, or until the corn mixture has thickened.

(continued)

To make the bean salad, mix together the fava beans, spinach, tomatoes, red onions, and the remaining ¼ cup corn. Add 1 tablespoon of the oil and a good squeeze of lime. Season with salt and pepper. Toss gently and set aside while you cook the fish.

In a 10-inch skillet, heat the remaining 1 tablespoon oil. Season the halibut on both sides generously with salt and pepper. Lay the fish in the pan and cook for 3 minutes, or until you get a nice sear on the bottom of the fish. Carefully turn the fillets over and cook for 2 minutes, or until cooked through.

To serve, spoon the corn zabaglione onto each plate, lay a piece of halibut across the center, and top with the fava salad.

MASTER THE BASICS:

SHUCKING FAVA BEANS

Also known as broad beans, the big, floppy green pods are a beloved spring vegetable popular in Mediterranean cuisine. Fresh fava beans have a creamy texture and lovely nutty taste. Although it's time-consuming, shucking fava beans is well worth the effort. They must first be removed from their outer pod and then slipped out of the tough skin that covers each bean.

Crab Cake with Lime-Thai Basil Aïoli and Cucumber Ribbon Salad

Recipe courtesy of Tracy Nailor

Tracy says, "Lifting off the top of the mystery box is always a nerve-racking experience—you never know what's going to be under there! For this challenge we only had one ingredient in the box: a spunky live crab! The judges made it very clear they wanted to be impressed and would not settle for plain steamed crab. After the initial panic of 'What in the world am I going to cook?' my mind clicked in to an Atlanta favorite—crab cakes. We were also given Thai basil, apple, cucumber, and lemongrass, so I put my own refreshing twist on the classic."

These succulent crab cakes are meaty, with very little mayo and filler so you can really taste the crab. The bright lime aïoli and tangy cucumber salad are the perfect complements to sweet crabmeat.

SERVES 4 TO 6

FOR THE CRAB CAKES

2 (2-pound) live Dungeness crab, or 1 pound jumbo lump crabmeat, picked through for shells (see Master the Basics: Cracking a Dungeness Crab, on page 68)

1 lemongrass stalk

2 limes

1 head of garlic, halved

1 teaspoon whole black peppercorns

1 tablespoon olive oil

1 shallot, minced

2 cloves garlic, minced

2 cups panko (Japanese) bread crumbs

8 fresh Thai basil leaves, finely chopped (see Chef Ingredient: Thai Basil, on page 108)

2 tablespoons mayonnaise

1 teaspoon dry mustard

½ teaspoon smoked paprika, plus more for garnish

1 large egg, beaten

Kosher salt and freshly ground black pepper

¼ cup grapeseed oil

FOR THE AÏOLI

1 large egg yolk

Juice of ½ lime

Pinch of cayenne pepper

3 fresh Thai basil leaves

1 cup grapeseed oil

Kosher salt and freshly ground black pepper

FOR THE CUCUMBER SALAD

1 English cucumber

1 Granny Smith apple

4 fresh Thai basil leaves, stacked, rolled, and cut into ribbons

Pinch of red-pepper flakes

1 tablespoon extra-virgin olive oil

1 tablespoon white vinegar

½ teaspoon kosher salt

¼ teaspoon freshly ground black pepper

(continued)

To make the crab cakes: Fill a large bowl with a tray of ice cubes and a couple of cups of water to create an ice bath.

Put the live crabs in the freezer for 20 minutes before cooking so that it is easier to handle them when putting them in the pot. Place a large pot of well-salted water over medium-high heat. Cut the lemongrass into 3-inch lengths, then bruise the lemongrass by hitting it a few times with the side of a knife to help release the fragrant, flavorful oils. Add the pieces to the pot. Halve 1 of the limes and squeeze the juice into the pot. Toss in both halves for extra flavor. Add the head of garlic and peppercorns. Bring the water to a rolling boil and carefully submerge the crabs in the water. Cover the pot to quickly bring the water back up to a boil. Cook the crabs for 12 to 15 minutes. The shell should turn bright red.

Put the crab in the ice water for several minutes to cool completely. Clean and crack the crab. Put the crabmeat in a mixing bowl and set aside.

Coat a small skillet with the olive oil and place over medium heat. When the oil is hot, add the shallot and minced garlic. Cook for 1 to 2 minutes. Remove from the heat and set aside to cool.

To the crabmeat, add 1 cup of the bread crumbs, basil, mayonnaise, dry mustard, paprika, egg, and the juice of the remaining lime. Scrape the cooled shallot and garlic into the bowl. Season with the salt and pepper. Fold the ingredients together gently but thoroughly, taking care not to mash the crabmeat. Using your hands, form the mixture into 4 crab cakes, roughly 1½ inches thick and about 4 inches in diameter. The crab cakes should be moist and just hold together. Put the crab cakes on a plate, cover with plastic wrap, and refrigerate while preparing the rest of the dish. Chilling allows the flavors to blend and the crab cakes to set so they hold together when fried.

To make the aïoli: Put the yolk in a blender with the lime juice, cayenne, and Thai basil leaves. Alternatively, mix in a bowl with a handheld electric mixer. With the motor running, pour in the oil and continue to blend until the mixture thickens to a mayonnaise consistency. Season with salt and pepper. Set aside in the refrigerator.

To make the salad: Using a vegetable peeler, peel off the skin of cucumber and discard. Keep peeling the cucumber into long ribbons into a bowl. Repeat this same process with the apple, stopping when you get to the core and turning the apple over to peel the other side. Add the basil, red-pepper flakes, olive oil, and vinegar. Season well with salt and pepper. Toss gently and set aside.

To cook the crab cakes, spread the remaining 1 cup bread crumbs out on a plate. Press both sides of the crab cakes in the bread crumbs to coat completely. Coat a large skillet with the ¼ cup grapeseed oil, swirling the pan to completely coat the bottom, and place over medium heat. Gently lay 2 of the cakes in the hot oil. Don't overcrowd the pan. Brown for 3 to 4 minutes on each side, turning gently with a spatula, and drain on paper towels. Repeat with the remaining crab cakes.

Serve the crab cakes with the aïoli and the cucumber ribbon salad on the side. Sprinkle paprika on the cakes and around the rim of the plates.

Roasted Pacific Rim Salmon Fillet with Chardonnay-Caper Sauce and Lemon Potatoes

 Recipe courtesy of MasterChef Kitchen

For the Wedding Challenge, the contestants were separated into teams and faced with the challenge of catering a wedding reception for 230 guests. Red Team Leader Sharone emphasized, "I'm a newlywed and recognize the food is a crucial part of the ceremony. The bride has been dreaming of this special day since she was a little girl—the stakes couldn't be any higher! We all were determined not let the bride and groom down."

The menu was set—a variation of surf-and-turf with roasted salmon and seared filet mignon. Simple and elegant, this satisfying roasted salmon hits all of the right notes with a zippy caper-wine sauce and lemon potatoes.

SERVES 4

FOR THE SALMON AND SAUCE

4 (6-ounce) salmon fillets, cut into 2 × 4-inch pieces (see Master the Basics: Preparing Salmon Fillets, on page 147)

Kosher salt and freshly ground black pepper

¼ cup olive oil, plus more for drizzling

1 shallot, thinly sliced

4 sprigs fresh thyme, leaves striped from the stem and chopped

½ cup Chardonnay

2 cups chopped fresh tomatoes (about 2 large)

2 tablespoons capers, drained and rinsed

FOR THE LEMON POTATOES

2 pounds fingerling potatoes, scrubbed, and halved lengthwise (about 25)

¼ cup olive oil

Zest and juice of 2 lemons

6 cloves garlic, chopped

¼ cup chopped fresh flat-leaf parsley, plus more for garnish

Kosher salt and freshly ground black pepper

1 lemon, cut into wedges

To make the salmon and sauce: Preheat the oven to 400°F. Season both sides of the salmon fillets with ½ teaspoon each salt and pepper. Drizzle a 9 × 13-inch baking dish with the oil and arrange the fish side by side in the pan.

Coat a frying pan with ¼ cup oil and place over medium heat. When the oil is hot, add the shallot and thyme. Cook and stir for 3 minutes, or until the shallot is translucent and fragrant. Season with salt and pepper. Pour in the wine and cook for 1 minute, or until the liquid is almost totally evaporated. Stir in the tomatoes and capers. Simmer, uncovered, stirring often, for 5 minutes, or until the sauce thickens slightly.

Pour the sauce over the salmon. Bake for 15 to 18 minutes, or until the fish is slightly firm but still pink inside, depending on how rare you like the center.

To make the potatoes: Preheat the oven to 400°F.

Put the potatoes in a baking dish and coat with the olive oil. Squeeze in the lemon juice and sprinkle in the zest. Scatter the garlic and parsley over the top. Season with ½ teaspoon each salt and pepper. Toss the potatoes to coat and spread them out in an even layer.

Roast for 1 hour, turning once or twice, until crispy and golden but fork-tender on the inside. Arrange the potatoes on a large plate, shower with chopped parsley, and sprinkle with coarse salt while they are hot.

To serve, spoon any liquid remaining from the salmon baking dish over the fish and serve with lemon wedges and lemon potatoes.

PREPARING SALMON FILLETS

To remove the skin from a fillet of fresh salmon, use a flexible fillet knife or a chef's knife. Cut a small piece from the tail end, to expose a flap of skin that you can grip firmly.

Grasp the end of the skin, with a towel if necessary, and insert the knife between the skin and flesh, angled slightly down toward the skin. Holding the tail end taut, slowly run the knife across the entire length of the fillet to remove the skin. If necessary, use a back-and-forth sawing motion as you ease the knife along between the skin and the flesh.

Salmon have a row of narrow pin bones running the length of the fillets, which must be removed by hand. Run your fingers down the middle of the fillet against the grain (from the wider end to the tail end) to locate the pin bones. Pull the pin bones out with clean tweezers or needle-nose pliers. Run your finger down the fillet again to make sure none are passed over. Slice the salmon into serving-size portions.

Saffron Butter-Poached Scorpion Fish with Israeli Couscous and Roasted Peppers

Recipe courtesy of Dave Miller

This field challenge began with the final five contestants shipping off to sea, where they had to catch the fish that they would later prepare for three top food critics. Dave says, "I hadn't been fishing since high school, when I went with a couple of my buddies—I never used to catch anything." But this time Dave had luck on his side—and caught a scorpion fish. "It's a fish that's better known in the Mediterranean," he says, "which is why I went with those flavors for my dish. The texture and flavor is very similar to mahi mahi."

After tasting Dave's fresh-caught dish, Gordon praised the amateur fisherman for his superior cooking skills and his near-perfect performance, remarking, "You raised the bar higher than we could have imagined."

SERVES 4

2 tablespoons olive oil

3 shallots, minced

2 cups Israeli couscous (see Chef Ingredient: Israeli Couscous on the opposite page)

Kosher salt and freshly ground black pepper

1 quart quality fish broth

1 each roasted red and yellow bell peppers, peeled and diced (see Master the Basics: Roasting Bell Peppers on page 99)

2 pounds cleaned scorpion fish or mahi mahi fillets, rinsed, and cut into 2 × 3-inch pieces (see Chef Ingredient: Scorpion Fish on the opposite page)

½ cup (1 stick) unsalted butter, cut into chunks

2 cloves garlic, minced

Pinch of saffron

Juice of ½ lemon

Fennel fronds, for garnish

1 teaspoon smoked sea salt, for garnish

Coat a pot with the oil and place over medium heat. When the oil is hot, add two-thirds of the shallots. Cook and stir for 2 minutes, or until soft. Add the couscous and cook, stirring, for 3 minutes, or until it browns slightly and smells nutty. Season with salt and pepper. Pour in the broth and bring to a boil. Reduce the heat to low. Cover and simmer for 8 minutes, or until the couscous is tender and the liquid is absorbed. Fold in the roasted peppers before serving. Keep warm.

Season the fish all over with a generous amount of salt and pepper. In a skillet large enough to hold the fish pieces in a single layer, melt the butter over low heat. Stir in the garlic, the remaining shallots, and saffron and cook until the butter becomes bright yellow. Lay the fish in the pan and cook slowly for 3 to 4 minutes, or until it begins to turn opaque. Spoon the butter over the fish to baste. Squeeze in the lemon juice and season with salt and pepper. Gently poach the fish in the melted butter and lemon juice for 3 minutes longer, or until the garlic is fragrant and the fish is moist and just cooked through. Taste and add more salt and pepper and a few drops of lemon juice, if desired.

Serve the fish on top of the couscous, drizzle the saffron butter on top and around the plate, and garnish with fennel fronds and a pinch of smoked sea salt.

CHEF INGREDIENTS:

Israeli Couscous

Also known as pearl couscous, Israeli couscous is significantly larger than its traditional granule cousin. It resembles a grain, like barley, but is considered pasta. Toasting lends the couscous a distinctive, nutty flavor and particularly satisfying mouth-feel, and it also seals in the starch, allowing the pearls to absorb liquid without falling apart.

Scorpion Fish

The scorpion fish is traditionally a very rustic, "poor man's" fish. It's called scorpion because of the poisonous spines that rise up along its dorsal fin, so exercise caution when handling this fish. While not fatal, the toxin can cause skin irritation. Mahi mahi or snapper makes a fine substitute.

Seared Mahi Mahi with Haricot Vert, Oven-Roasted Tomatoes, and Kalamata Olive Purée

Recipe courtesy of Graham Elliot

If he were a MasterChef contestant instead of a judge, what dish would Chef Graham Elliot whip up for a fishing challenge? "I love creating dishes around fresh seafood," he says. "The biggest challenge is seasoning correctly and making sure you don't overcook the fish. The fish is the lead singer of the band. You want to put the rest of the group together to make the delicacy of the fish really sing, without overpowering. For the accompaniments on this dish, I tried to stay with ingredients that pair well with citrus. This would ultimately let the fish be the dominant flavor while creating depth with the other components."

SERVES 4

1 cup pitted kalamata olives, rinsed

¼ cup fresh orange juice

1 cup plus 5 tablespoons extra-virgin olive oil

1 pint cherry tomatoes

Kosher salt and freshly ground black pepper

4 (5-ounce) mahi-mahi or red snapper fillets, about 1 inch thick

2 navel oranges, cut into segments (see Master the Basics: Segmenting Citrus, on page 53)

¼ cup fresh chervil or flat-leaf parsley leaves

8 sprigs fresh chives, thinly sliced

1 pound haricot vert (French green beans), blanched and sliced (see Master the Basics: Blanching, on page 132)

Preheat the oven to 400°F.

Combine the olives and orange juice in a blender. Blend on high speed for 2 minutes. Slowly drizzle in 1 cup oil while the blender is running. It is very important that the oil is added slowly, otherwise the mixture will separate. Once combined, set the olive purée aside at room temperature.

Put the tomatoes in a baking dish, drizzle with 2 tablespoons of the oil, and season with salt and pepper. Bake for 15 minutes, or until soft.

Meanwhile, season the fillets on both sides with 1 teaspoon each salt and pepper. Coat a large ovenproof or cast-iron skillet with 2 tablespoons of the oil and place over medium-high heat. In order to get a proper sear on the fish, the pan needs to be hot. Lay the fish in the pan and let it sear without moving the fillets around. Cook for 5 minutes at a hard sear and then transfer the skillet to the oven for 5 minutes. Remove from the oven and carefully turn the fish with a spatula. Let the fish finish cooking in the hot pan, out of the oven and off the heat, for 2 minutes.

To make the salad, combine the orange segments, chervil leaves, and chives in a bowl. Drizzle with the remaining 1 tablespoon oil and season with salt and pepper.

To serve, smear a spoonful of the olive purée on the base of the plate. Pile the green beans and oven-roasted tomatoes on top and lay a fish fillet across. Garnish with the orange salad.

Oysters on the Half Shell with Classic Mignonette

 Recipe courtesy of MasterChef **Kitchen**

Oysters have long been considered an aphrodisiac. In fact, Casanova supposedly started each day by consuming 50 of them. Oysters have trace amounts of zinc that give the body stamina. Perhaps with all he consumed, there is indeed a connection to his fabled prowess!

When it comes to eating fresh oysters, less is more. For the best-tasting oysters, shuck them, serve them, and eat them immediately. If you eat oysters at home regularly, it's a good idea to invest in a couple of oyster knives, which are inexpensive and built for the sole purpose of shucking. Mignonette, a classic accompaniment to raw oysters, is a vinegar-based condiment made with shallots. The bite of black pepper and the acidity and brightness of vinegar pair well with the briny shellfish.

SERVES 4, MAKES ½ CUP SAUCE

½ cup champagne or red wine vinegar

1 shallot, finely minced

1 teaspoon coarsely ground black pepper

1 teaspoon finely chopped fresh flat-leaf parsley

24 fresh oysters, such as Kumamoto, bluepoint, or Hama Hama (see Master the Basics: Shucking Oysters, on page 154)

Crushed ice or rock salt

Lemon wedges

Hot sauce, such as Tabasco

In a small bowl, combine the vinegar, shallot, pepper, and parsley and mix with a fork. Cover and chill the mignonette for at least 1 hour or up to the day before you plan to serve, to allow the flavors to come together.

Shuck the oysters as directed on page 154.

Spoon a few drops of mignonette, lemon juice, or hot sauce on the raw oysters before eating them. To eat a raw oyster, tip the shell into your mouth, being careful to not spill the flavorful liquid surrounding the meat. Oyster lovers are divided as to whether it's better to chew or simply slurp it down, but there's really no wrong way to do it.

SHUCKING OYSTERS

Scrub the oysters under cold water with a stiff brush to remove the dirt, especially in the hinge area where mud has a tendency to get trapped. Fold a dish towel over several times to create a square. This will steady the oysters as you shuck them and also protect your hand.

Put the towel on a flat surface and place the oyster on top, with the flat side facing up and the hinge (the pointy bit where the top half of the shell meets the bottom half) facing you. Have a small bowl handy to catch the delicious juice.

Fold part of the towel back over the top of the oyster to keep it in place. Insert the tip of an oyster knife as far into the hinge as it will go. Don't jab it in there or you could break the shell.

With gentle force, twist and wriggle the knife back and forth to pry the shell open. Put some muscle into it, but be careful—this is where you can cut yourself.

Slide the knife along the top lid to cut the muscle away, pull the shell off, and discard it. Turn the oyster around and slide the knife underneath the oyster to detach it completely, but leave it in its shell. Clean away any bits of shell that may have chipped off. Be sure not to spill out the briny liquid.

Nestle the oysters in a bed of crushed ice or rock salt to keep them steady. Serve with lemon wedges, hot sauce, and mignonette.

Tips for Buying and Storing Oysters

- Oysters are perfectly safe to eat year-round. The old rule about only eating oysters in months that have the letter *r* in their names has more to do with the way the oysters reproduce than with safety. It is said that oysters are best when consumed in these months and in winter months because cold water produces tastier oysters.

- Oysters are sold live either by the dozen or by weight. Buy oysters from a reliable fish purveyor that sells through its supply every few days. It's a good idea to purchase a few more than you plan on serving; one or two might break, or you might get a dud.

- Fresh oysters should not smell "fishy," only like fresh seawater. If an oyster is alive, it does not have a fishy odor.

- Select oysters that are heavy, firmly closed, and don't sound hollow when tapped. If an oyster is open (which it shouldn't be), it should snap shut TIGHT if you tap on the shell. That means it's alive. Do not buy or eat dead oysters—or you are sure to suffer a stomachache.

- Size does matter—the deeper the cup of the lower shell, the more meat the oyster contains.

- Oysters should be stored and served cup side down, so they are sitting in their own fluids.

- If you are not going to use the oysters immediately, they need to be carefully stored to keep them alive. Wrap oysters loosely in a damp towel and set them in a bowl (ice isn't necessary), and put them in the fridge for a day or so. They will continue to live and stay fresh if stored this way. DO NOT put them in water or in a sealed plastic bag, as they will suffocate.

Types of Oysters

- **Atlantic/Eastern oysters:** Varieties include bluepoint, Wellfleet, and Malpeque. In general, these oysters are considered to be firmer, somewhat better for eating raw and are really briny.

- **European/flat oysters:** Varieties include Belon. They are generally round in shape and have a pleasant metallic taste.

- **Kumamoto oysters:** These small, nonintimidating oysters are every beginner's favorite. With their distinctive frilly black shell, they have the right amount of salinity and a sweet, mild flavor.

- **Olympia oysters:** These oysters are native to the Pacific Northwest, often from Puget Sound outside of Seattle. They are tiny but offer big, assertive flavor.

- **Pacific/Japanese oysters:** Varieties include Hama Hama and Hog Island. They are generally sweet, with melon, cucumber, or mineral nuances.

Steamed Lobster with Drawn Butter

 Recipe courtesy of MasterChef **Kitchen**

Steaming is a great way to cook lobster without fear of overcooking its delicate meat. Knowing how to properly crack and eat a lobster is as impressive a skill as being able to cook one. Special equipment needed for cooking and consuming lobsters are kitchen shears, tongs, crackers, bibs, and, of course, napkins to wipe your chin! Making drawn butter is easier than you might think—it's just a matter of heating and straining it to remove the milk solids.

SERVES 4

1 tablespoon kosher salt

½ bunch fresh thyme

4 bay leaves

2 lemons, plus wedges for serving

4 live lobsters (about 2 pounds each)

1 cup (2 sticks) unsalted butter

1 tablespoon finely chopped fresh flat-leaf parsley

1 tablespoon finely chopped fresh basil leaves

Fill a large steamer or soup pot with about 2 inches of water and add the salt, thyme, bay leaves, and the juice of 1 lemon. Add the squeezed halves for extra flavor. Bring to a boil over medium heat.

Place the lobsters in the steamer basket or directly in the pot, cover, and allow to steam for 15 minutes. The lobster shells will be bright red and the tail will be curled when they are done. Remove the lobsters from the pot and cool to room temperature. Chill thoroughly in the fridge before cracking open.

Meanwhile, heat the butter in a small pot over low heat. Warm it up gently so the milk solids begin to cook and sink to the bottom of the pot. Keep a close watch because once the milk solids collect and fall, they burn easily. Strain the clear butter into a small serving cup, leaving the solids behind. Squeeze in the juice of the remaining lemon, and stir in the parsley and basil.

Serve lobster with the drawn butter and lemon wedges. (See Master the Basics: Cracking a Lobster, on page 158.)

CRACKING A LOBSTER

1. Twist off both of the claws from the body. Separate the claw and knuckle by snapping it like a twig.

2. Pull off the small legs from the body, and remove the meat with a lobster fork or suck out the meat and juice. Turn the body over and scoop out the meat from the pockets. (There may be a green substance called tamale, which is actually the liver and is considered a delicacy.)

3. Use a lobster or nutcracker to crack the large claws just below the tip.

4. Pull off the shell and remove the meat in one piece.

5. Twist the head and tail of the lobster in opposite directions, separating the tail from the body.

6. Break off the tail fins. Stick a fork inside the tail to pull out the meat in one piece, taking care not to tear any of the flesh.

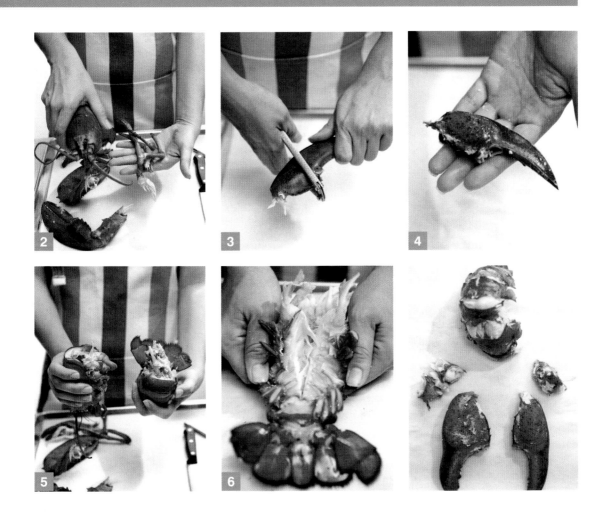

Shrimp Cocktail

 Recipe courtesy of MasterChef **Kitchen**

Shrimp Cocktail is a classic appetizer that is pretty easy to make and sure to impress your guests. The cocktail sauce can be made a few days in advance and kept covered in the refrigerator.

SERVES 4

FOR THE SHRIMP

1 tablespoon kosher salt

1 lemon, halved, plus more for serving

2 bay leaves

1 handful fresh thyme

1 handful fresh flat-leaf parsley

1 pound jumbo shrimp, with shells and tails on (see Master the Basics: Peeling and Deveining Shrimp, on page 162)

FOR THE COCKTAIL SAUCE

½ cup ketchup

½ small onion, finely minced

1 tablespoon grated fresh or prepared horseradish

1 tablespoon Worcestershire sauce

Juice of 1 lemon

1 teaspoon hot sauce, such as Tabasco

1 teaspoon celery seed

Kosher salt and freshly ground black pepper

To make the shrimp: Fill a large pot with about 2 quarts of water, add the salt, and squeeze in the lemon juice. Toss in the lemon halves for extra flavor. Add the bay leaves, thyme, and parsley. Bring to a boil over medium-high heat and simmer for 5 minutes to infuse the water with the aromatics.

Reduce the heat to medium-low and add the shrimp. Simmer, uncovered, for 3 to 5 minutes, or until the shrimp are bright pink and begin to curl. Drain the shrimp and immediately rinse in cold water. Chill thoroughly before peeling.

To make the cocktail sauce: In a small bowl, combine the ketchup, onion, horseradish, Worcestershire, lemon juice, hot sauce, and celery seed. Season with salt and pepper. Chill the cocktail sauce for 30 minutes, if time allows.

Serve the shrimp with cocktail sauce and lemon wedges.

PEELING AND DEVEINING SHRIMP

To peel shrimp, grasp the legs on the underside and pull the peel away from the meat. Remove the tail, if desired. The shells can be used to make a terrific broth.

Shrimp are edible without being deveined, though many people prefer to eat deveined shrimp. The dark "vein" that runs through a shrimp's body is actually its intestinal tract. As such, it contains some waste from the shrimp's body.

To devein a shrimp, use a paring knife to make an incision down the curved backside of the shrimp, following the dark line of the intestinal tract. Use the tip of the knife to scrape out the gray vein or pull it out in one piece and rinse the shrimp under cool water.

MEAT

Pork Tenderloin
with Braised Fennel and
Spaetzle in Orange Sauce

Recipe courtesy of Sheena Zadeh

Sheena says, "I thought I wanted to be doctor. What I discovered is my background in science has given me a real appreciation for the chemistry of cooking. I love to see what happens when you mix ingredients together."

As she nervously introduced her signature dish, the judges joked that she sounded like a foodie . . . but could she cook like one? While the braised fennel and delicate spaetzle coated with orange sauce hit the right notes, the judges felt her pork tenderloin was a little dry. "If the pork was just cooked 1 minute less, it would have been a perfect dish," said judge Joe Bastianich. Let that be a lesson to you—don't overcook your pork!

SERVES 4

1 cup all-purpose flour

Kosher salt and freshly ground black pepper

½ teaspoon freshly grated nutmeg

2 large eggs

½ cup half-and-half

5 tablespoons extra-virgin olive oil

2 fennel bulbs, quartered, core removed

1 quart Chicken Broth (page 242), or quality store-bought

2 shallots, minced

2 tablespoons red wine vinegar

1 cup orange juice

½ cup (1 stick) unsalted butter

1 (2-pound) pork tenderloin, cut into ½-inch-thick medallions

6 sprigs fresh thyme

2 tablespoons chopped fresh flat-leaf parsley

In a large bowl, combine the flour, 1 teaspoon salt, ½ teaspoon pepper, and nutmeg. In another mixing bowl, whisk the eggs and half-and-half together. Make a well in the center of the dry ingredients and pour in the egg mixture. Gradually draw in the flour from the sides and combine well. The dough should be sticky and thick. Take care not to overwork. Let the dough rest for 10 to 15 minutes to allow the gluten to relax.

Bring a large pot of well-salted water to a boil. To form the spaetzle, hold a large-holed colander or potato ricer over the simmering water and push the dough through the holes with a spatula or spoon. Do this in batches so you don't overcrowd the pot. Cook 1 to 2 minutes, or until the spaetzle floats to the surface, stirring gently to prevent sticking. Dump the spaetzle into a colander in the sink and rinse quickly with cool water. Set aside. The spaetzle may be made up to 1 hour ahead.

(continued)

Coat a wide skillet with 2 tablespoons of the oil and place over medium-low heat. When the oil is hot, lay the fennel pieces in the pan, cut side down, and season generously with salt and pepper. Cook for 3 to 4 minutes, or until the fennel begins to brown. Pour in the broth to cover the fennel and gently simmer for 15 to 20 minutes, or until tender.

Coat a small pot with 1 tablespoon of the oil and place over medium heat. When the oil is hot, add the shallots. Cook and stir for 1 minute, until translucent. Pour in the vinegar and stir to release the brown bits at the bottom of the pot. Pour in the orange juice. Simmer gently for 5 to 10 minutes to reduce the liquid. Stir in 2 tablespoons of the butter to finish the sauce. Cover to keep warm.

Place a large skillet over medium heat and add the remaining 2 tablespoons oil. When the oil is hot, lay the pork medallions in the pan and scatter the thyme sprigs on top. Cook for 1 to 2 minutes, or until you get a nice sear on the meat. Turn the pork over and add 2 tablespoons of the butter. When the butter has melted, baste the pork with the thyme butter. Cook for 1 to 2 minutes (pork dries out easily). Remove from the heat and keep warm.

To finish the spaetzle, melt the remaining 4 tablespoons butter in the same skillet over medium heat. Add the spaetzle and toss to coat. Cook the spaetzle for 1 to 2 minutes to give the noodles some color, and then sprinkle with the chopped parsley and season with salt and pepper.

To serve, divide the spaetzle among 4 plates, lay a few slices of pork on top, and drizzle with the orange sauce. Arrange 2 wedges of braised fennel on the side. Garnish with the butter-cooked thyme sprigs.

Southern-Fried Pork Chop with Coleslaw

Recipe courtesy of Whitney Miller

For each Mystery Box Challenge, the contestants were given a box of ingredients and the challenge of creating an outstanding dish in 45 minutes using some or all of those ingredients. In the first Mystery Box Challenge, the amateur chefs lifted the wooden box in front of them to find 14 ingredients: a pork chop, bread, cabbage, Granny Smith apple, tomato, lemon, flat-leaf parsley, cinnamon stick, chocolate, eggs, sugar, butter, cream, and a little bottle of brandy.

A nervous Whitney revealed, "I've never cooked a pork chop before!" Apparently she had beginner's luck on her side. She was shocked—and thrilled—to hear Joe refer to her simple dish as "an orchestra of flavors."

SERVES 4

FOR THE COLESLAW

½ head green cabbage, shredded (about 6 cups)

1 Granny Smith apple, cut into matchsticks (about 2 cups)

2 tablespoons chopped fresh flat-leaf parsley, plus more for garnish

¼ cup whole milk

Zest, finely grated, and juice of 1 lemon

2 teaspoons sugar

½ teaspoon kosher salt

½ teaspoon freshly ground black pepper

FOR THE PORK CHOPS

4 slices (1 inch thick) day-old white bread, crusts removed and cubed

½ teaspoon ground cinnamon

Kosher salt and freshly ground black pepper

2 large eggs

4 (8-ounce) bone-in pork loin chops

2 tablespoons olive oil

2 tablespoons unsalted butter

1 cinnamon stick, quartered, for garnish

To make the coleslaw: In a large bowl, mix the cabbage, apple, and parsley. In a separate bowl, whisk together the milk, lemon, sugar, salt, and pepper. Pour over the slaw and toss thoroughly to coat. Set aside in the refrigerator to develop the flavors.

To make the pork chops: Preheat the oven to 400°F.

In a food processor, pulse the bread cubes until they crumble into soft bread crumbs roughly the size of peppercorns. There should be about 1 cup. Pour the bread crumbs into a wide bowl; add the cinnamon, season with ¼ teaspoon each salt and pepper; and combine thoroughly to distribute the spices. In another bowl, whisk the eggs, add 1 tablespoon of water, and beat to combine.

(continued)

Season the pork chops generously on all sides with salt and pepper. You should see the seasoning on the meat. Dip each chop into the eggs and then dredge in the bread crumb mixture.

Heat the oil and butter in an ovenproof skillet or cast-iron pan over medium heat. Put the pork chops in the pan, working in batches if necessary, and cook for 3 to 5 minutes per side, or until nicely browned. Transfer the skillet to the oven and bake for 5 to 7 minutes, or until the meat bears only a light trace of pink. The internal temperature should be 150°F. Remove the pork chops to a cutting board to rest for 5 minutes, so the juices settle back into the meat.

To serve, scoop out a portion of the slaw into a small ramekin and invert onto each plate. Cut the pork chops on the bias into ½-inch slices, and layer them in an overlapping pattern in front of the slaw. Season with freshly ground black pepper and garnish with a cinnamon stick piece and chopped parsley.

Apple-Raisin Stuffed Pork Loin with Natural Pan Jus

Recipe courtesy of the Blue Team (Mike, Jake, Lee, Tracy, Tony, Sheetal)

When the 12 remaining contestants were divided into two teams to cook for the Marines at Camp Pendleton military base, the challenge was daunting: Each team had to prepare a memorable meal for 400 Marines about to depart for active duty, as well as for the families they would soon be leaving. As Blue Team member Jake said, "We literally have an army to feed! And we can't let down our nation's greatest."

The Blue Team's hearty and heartfelt dish satisfied the Marines and secured a most gratifying win for the team members.

SERVES 8 TO 10

½ cup dry white wine, such as Sauvignon Blanc

½ cup golden raisins

¼ cup extra-virgin olive oil

1 onion, chopped

1 Granny Smith apple, peeled and diced

Kosher salt and freshly ground black pepper

½ cup chopped raw almonds

2 cloves garlic, minced

¼ cup chopped fresh flat-leaf parsley

2 tablespoons chopped fresh basil

1 (4-pound) pork loin

½ cup Chicken Broth (page 242), or quality store-bought

Heat the wine in a small pot or microwave until hot. Pour over the raisins, cover with plastic wrap, and allow to sit and plump up for 10 minutes while preparing the rest of the ingredients.

Coat a large skillet with 1 tablespoon of the oil and place over medium heat. When the oil is hot, add the onion and apple. Season with salt and pepper. Cook and stir for 2 minutes, or until the onion and apple begin to soften. Add the almonds and garlic. Continue to cook, tossing, for 3 minutes, or until the almonds are lightly toasted and the garlic is fragrant. Scrape the mixture into a bowl. No need to wipe out the skillet—it will be used again to sear the pork.

Drain the wine from the raisins and reserve. Mix the macerated raisins, parsley, and basil into the apple mixture. Season again with salt and pepper. Toss to combine and set the stuffing aside.

Using a sharp knife, cut the pork loin lengthwise down the middle and open it up flat like a book. Season the surface of the pork loin generously with salt and pepper and drizzle with the remaining 3 tablespoons oil. Evenly distribute the apple mixture inside the pork and pat down. Push the loin back together to close up the stuffing.

Cut kitchen twine into 6 (12-inch) pieces. Tie the roast securely with the twine but not so tight that you squeeze out the stuffing. Season all over with salt and pepper. The pork loin may be stuffed and tied a day in advance, if desired.

Preheat the oven to 400°F.

Return the skillet to medium-high heat. When the pan is hot, lay the tenderloin in the pan and sear on both sides for 2 minutes each to form a crust.

Set the pork loin in a roasting pan and roast for 1 hour, or until an instant-read thermometer registers 155°F. Remove the pork loin to a cutting board and allow to rest for 10 minutes. Put the roasting pan on two burners over medium heat. Add the reserved wine from the raisins, stirring with a wooden spoon to scrape up all the brown bits at the bottom of the pan. Stir in the broth and season with salt and pepper, if necessary. Pour the pan sauce from the roasting pan into a gravy boat.

To serve, cut off the kitchen twine and cut the pork into ½-inch-thick slices. Arrange on a serving platter and serve with the jus on the side.

Eclectic Surf and Turf (Steak Spiedini with Charred Asparagus and Seared Scallops with Pea Purée)

Recipe courtesy of Jake Gandolfo

When it comes to rough-and-tumble Jake Gandolfo, you can't judge a book by its cover. The tattooed construction worker from Santa Cruz, California, came to *MasterChef* looking to trade in his toolbox for a set of knives. He told the judges, "I am super passionate about food and cooking and want the opportunity to learn from the best."

For his signature dish, Jake cooked his variation on surf and turf: rolled steak with delicate scallops and pea purée. Gordon was not wowed, but Graham Elliot defended Jake. "Cooking is similar to construction," he explained. "You need a strong foundation to build upon. This dish shows a lot of promise. Deep down under that construction worker, there's a chef."

SERVES 4

FOR THE TURF

4 tablespoons extra-virgin olive oil

1 cup freshly grated Parmesan cheese (3 ounces)

6 fresh basil leaves, chopped

6 sprigs fresh flat-leaf parsley, chopped

2 cloves garlic, minced

Kosher salt and freshly ground black pepper

4 (5-ounce) skirt or loin flap steaks

1 cup panko (Japanese) bread crumbs

1 bunch thin asparagus, about 14 to 16 spears

1 scallion, root trimmed

FOR THE SURF

3 tablespoons unsalted butter

1 shallot, minced

2 cloves garlic, minced

2 cups shelled fresh sweet peas or frozen and thawed

1 cup Vegetable Broth (page 243), or quality store-bought

8 fresh mint leaves

Kosher salt and freshly ground black pepper

12 large sea scallops (about 12 ounces)

To make the turf: Brush an outdoor gas or charcoal grill or grill pan with oil to prevent sticking, and preheat to medium-high.

In a small bowl, combine the cheese, basil, parsley, and garlic. Season with salt and pepper. Set aside.

Lay the meat out on a cutting board and pound to ¼-inch thickness, if necessary—in most cases, skirt and flap steaks are fairly thin. Brush the meat with 1 tablespoon of the oil. Sprinkle the cheese mixture evenly over

(continued)

the steak. Tightly roll the steak away from you to enclose the filling. Secure the ends with a skewer, weaving it in and out through the meat from one end to the other. Rub 1 tablespoon of the oil on the outside of the meat.

Spread the bread crumbs on a shallow platter and season with salt and pepper. Carefully roll the steak in the bread crumbs to cover all sides.

Grill the steaks, turning often, for 8 to 10 minutes, or until browned all over and an instant-read thermometer registers 125°F for medium-rare. Remove the steak to a cutting board and let rest for 5 minutes.

Put the asparagus and scallion in a bowl, drizzle with the remaining 2 tablespoons olive oil, season with salt and pepper, and toss to coat. Peel the scallion from top to bottom into 4 long strands. Gather 3 or 4 asparagus spears together and tie in a bundle with a green onion strand. Lay the spears on the grill and cook for 2 to 3 minutes, or until nicely charred on all sides.

To make the surf: Put a pot over medium heat and add 1 tablespoon of butter. When the butter has melted, add the shallot and cook, stirring, for 1 to 2 minutes, or until softened. Add the garlic to the pot and sweat for 30 seconds. Add the peas and cook, stirring frequently, for 3 minutes. Pour in the broth and bring the liquid to a boil. Reduce the heat to medium-low and simmer for 5 minutes, or until the peas are tender.

Remove from the heat, add the mint, and season with salt and pepper. Purée with an immersion blender or carefully transfer the mixture to a standing blender. Process on low speed for 1 to 2 minutes, or until the peas form a smooth purée. Be careful blending the hot ingredients—make sure to hold the lid securely with a thick kitchen towel. Cover the pea purée to keep warm.

Season the scallops on both sides with salt and pepper. Coat a small skillet with the remaining 2 tablespoons butter and place over medium heat. When the butter has melted, lay the scallops in the pan. Cook the scallops, without moving them around, for 2 to 3 minutes to form a nice golden sear. Gently turn the scallops over to cook the other side for 1 minute, or until the scallops are firm but still moist and supple. Remove from the heat.

To serve, spoon the pea purée onto one of the plates. Remove the skewers from the rolled steak and slice into 5-inch pinwheels. Place one pinwheel on top of the pea puree. Add several scallops to the plate. Top with an asparagus bundle.

Grilled Skirt Steaks with Savory Barbecue Sauce and Bacon-Potato Au Gratin

Recipe courtesy of the Red Team (Sharone, Dave, Jenna, Whitney, Faruq)

When the contestants were faced with the challenge of feeding a few hundred Marines, the Red Team chose to prepare a hearty, all-American meal of steak and potatoes to satisfy the troops.

Graham Elliot asked the contestants to rise to the occasion, revealing that this challenge resonated with him on a personal level. "My dad served in the Navy, and I grew up on military bases," he shared. "These guys are willing to put their lives on the line and deserve the best. Make this one count, and give them a meal to remember."

SERVES 4

FOR THE SKIRT STEAKS

4 pounds skirt steaks

½ cup plus 2 tablespoons extra-virgin olive oil

1 onion, diced

3 cloves garlic, minced

Kosher salt and freshly ground black pepper

½ cup apple cider vinegar

1 teaspoon balsamic vinegar

1 tablespoon Worcestershire sauce

¼ cup dark brown sugar, packed

1 cup ketchup

1 teaspoon smoked paprika

1 teaspoon hot sauce, such as Tabasco

Pinch of red-pepper flakes

FOR THE BACON-POTATO AU GRATIN

4 bacon slices

1 tablespoon unsalted butter

5 cloves garlic, minced

3 cups heavy cream

¼ teaspoon cayenne pepper

1 teaspoon kosher salt

1 teaspoon freshly ground black pepper

4 scallions, white and green parts, chopped

2 pounds baking (Idaho) potatoes, unpeeled (about 5 potatoes)

1 cup shredded Monterey Jack cheese

1 cup shredded sharp Cheddar cheese

To make the steaks: Put the steaks in a large baking dish and coat with ½ cup oil. Marinate the steak for 30 minutes at room temperature, turning to coat both sides.

Coat a large pot with 2 tablespoons oil and place over medium-low heat. When the oil is hot, add the onion and garlic. Cook and stir for 3 minutes to soften. Season with salt and pepper. Add the vinegars, Worcestershire, sugar, ketchup, paprika, hot sauce, and red-pepper flakes. Cook and stir for 15 minutes, until the sauce is thick. Set aside to cool to room temperature.

Heat a grill pan over high heat. Remove the steak from the oil and season generously with salt and pepper. Grill the steaks on one side for 3 to 4 minutes, or until slightly charred. Turn the steaks over and cook for 3 to 4 minutes longer, or to medium-rare doneness. Let the steak rest 5 minutes, then slice against the grain into ¼-inch-thick slices.

To make the au gratin: Preheat the oven to 300°F.

Place a large pot over medium-low heat and fry the bacon until crisp. Remove from the pan with a slotted spoon and drain on paper towels. Crumble and set aside.

Add the butter to the bacon fat in the pan. When it has melted, mix in the garlic and give it a quick stir with a wooden spoon to soften. Cook for 2 to 3 minutes, or until soft but not brown. Add the heavy cream, cayenne, salt, and pepper. Bring to a gentle simmer. Remove from the heat and add half of the scallions, reserving the rest for garnish.

Thinly slice the potatoes, approximately ¼ inch thick, using a chef's knife, mandoline, or processor attachment blade. Add the potatoes to the cream as quickly as possible to prevent the potatoes from discoloring. Toss, rotating the potatoes from the bottom to the top, to evenly coat.

Using your hands, layer the potatoes on the bottom of a 9 × 13-inch baking dish. Sprinkle with the cheeses and bacon and repeat with two more layers. Pour any remaining cream on top of the potatoes.

Bake the potatoes, uncovered, for 1 hour and 15 minutes, or until they are cooked through and the top begins to brown. Remove from the oven. The gratin will look a little soupy but will firm up as it cools. Let it rest for 10 to 15 minutes before cutting and serving. The resting time allows the potatoes to reabsorb some of the cream and helps the gratin hold its shape. Sprinkle the remaining scallions on top for garnish.

To serve, layer the meat in an overlapping pattern on a platter and spoon the barbecue sauce across the top. Serve with the potatoes on the side.

Chef Graham's Texas-Style Chili

Recipe courtesy of Graham Elliot

For the first Pressure Test, the Red Team was required to use their senses of sight, smell, and taste to identify the 20 ingredients used in Chef Graham's Texas-Style Chili. This rich, satisfying dish will soon become your go-to chili recipe.

SERVES 6

2 pounds top sirloin, cut into large cubes

2 pounds boneless pork shoulder, cut into large cubes

2 tablespoons ground cumin

2 tablespoons ground ancho chili powder

1 tablespoon kosher salt

¼ cup vegetable oil, plus more if needed

10 cloves garlic, chopped

6 celery stalks, coarsely chopped

1 large onion, coarsely chopped

1 green bell pepper, halved, cored, seeded, and chopped

1 jalapeño chile pepper, sliced (wear plastic gloves when handling)

1 can (28 ounces) whole tomatoes

1 can (15½ ounces) beef broth

1 bottle (12 ounces) beer, preferably smoked porter or dark lager

4 chipotles in adobo, chopped

2 cinnamon sticks

1 small bunch fresh oregano, coarsely chopped

1 can (15 ounces) pinto beans, rinsed and drained

Juice of 2 limes

1 small bunch fresh cilantro, coarsely chopped

Put the beef and pork in a large bowl. Sprinkle with the cumin, chili powder, and salt, tossing to coat.

Coat a large stockpot with the oil and place over medium heat. When the oil is hot, add the beef and pork. Do this in batches, if necessary, to avoid overcrowding the pot. Brown on all sides. Remove the meat to a side platter and keep the pot on the heat.

Add more oil to the drippings in the pot, if necessary. Add the garlic, celery, onion, bell pepper, and jalapeño. Cook and stir for 10 minutes, or until the vegetables soften.

Return the meat to the pot. Place the tomatoes (with juice) in a large bowl and hand-crush them until chunky. Add the tomatoes to the pot along with the broth, beer, chipotles, cinnamon, and oregano. Simmer, uncovered, for 2½ hours, or until the meat is fork-tender and comes apart with no resistance. Add the beans and cook for 30 minutes longer, stirring occasionally. In the last 5 minutes of cooking, add the lime juice and cilantro.

Beef Tataki with Passion Fruit Ponzu Sauce and Fried Lotus Chips

Recipe courtesy of Mike Kim

Tataki is a style of Japanese cooking in which meat is briefly seared and thinly sliced. In Mike's recipe, tender beef is the perfect backdrop for a drizzling of tangy ponzu sauce, made from passion fruit, citrus, and soy. When asked what inspired his "romantic" Invention Test, Mike replied, "I love everybody!"

And apparently, everybody loves Mike, who received rave reviews from the judges. Joe praised the dish as "beautiful to look at" and remarked that "the bright flavor of passion fruit really comes through."

SERVES 4

½ cup soy sauce

½ cup balsamic vinegar

Juice of 3 tangerines

Juice of 2 limes

Juice of 1 lemon

10 passion fruits, halved (see Master the Basics: Passion Fruit, on page 192)

2 tablespoons olive oil

2 (5-to-6-ounce) pieces beef tenderloin

Kosher salt and freshly ground black pepper

¼ cup corn oil

1 (6-to-8-ounce) lotus root, peeled and sliced paper-thin with a sharp knife or mandoline

2 cups baby arugula, loosely packed

3 kumquats, thinly sliced, for garnish

1 packet (4 ounces) edible flowers, for garnish

In a medium pot, combine the soy sauce and balsamic vinegar and cook over medium-low heat for 8 minutes, to reduce by half.

Meanwhile, combine the citrus juices in a bowl. Set a fine-mesh strainer over the bowl. Scrape out the pulp of the passion fruit with a spoon, and press it through the strainer to remove the seeds. You should get about ½ cup of juice. Pour the citrus-passion fruit mixture into the pot with the soy and vinegar. Simmer for 10 to 15 minutes, or until the liquid reduces by about half and is syrupy.

In a large, preferably cast-iron skillet, heat the olive oil over medium-high heat. Season the tenderloins on all sides with 1 teaspoon each salt and pepper. When the oil is hot, lay the meat in the pan and sear on each side for 1 to 2 minutes, for rare. Remove to a clean cutting board to rest briefly.

Meanwhile, in a large skillet with high sides, heat the corn oil until rippling. Using tongs, carefully arrange the lotus slices in the pan, in a single layer, working in batches if necessary. Fry for 2 minutes per side, or until golden brown and crispy. Remove the fried lotus to a plate lined with paper towel. Season with salt and pepper while still hot.

To serve, pile a generous handful of arugula to form a large bed on each plate. Slice the tenderloin into $\frac{1}{4}$-inch strips and layer in an overlapping pattern on the arugula. Surround the beef with kumquat slices. Drizzle the passion fruit ponzu sauce on top and around the plate. Top with 3 or 4 lotus chips, and scatter a few edible flowers on the rim of the plate. Serve with crispy lotus chips and any extra ponzu sauce on the side, for dipping.

Truck Stop Meat Loaf Burger with Spicy Barbecue Sauce

Recipe courtesy of the Red Team (Sharone, Mike, Dave, Sheetal, Slim)

For the second MasterChef team challenge—the Burger Challenge—the amateur chefs faced yet another tough task: creating the perfect burger for a group of truckers at a roadside diner. The Red Team's double-comfort food dish—a meat loaf burger—got the highest marks, winning over the truckers and the judges.

Graham Elliot advises, "If you want a burger with superior flavor, you need to freshly grind the meat yourself—it's as simple as that. The process is not only easier than most people think, but also makes the moistest and most flavorful burgers. If you don't have a meat grinder attachment for your food processor, ask your local butcher to grind the meat for you."

SERVES 6, MAKES 1 CUP SAUCE

FOR THE BARBECUE SAUCE

2 tablespoons bacon drippings

1 tablespoon olive oil

½ small onion, minced

Kosher salt and freshly ground black pepper

4 cloves garlic, minced

1 small jalapeño chile pepper, seeded if desired (wear plastic gloves when handling)

2 tablespoons light brown sugar, loosely packed

2 chipotle chiles in adobo, chopped

½ cup Beef Broth (page 244), or quality store-bought

½ cup white wine vinegar

½ cup ketchup

1 tablespoon tomato paste

FOR THE BURGERS

¼ cup dry bread crumbs

½ cup Beef Broth (page 244), or quality store-bought

1 large egg

1 tablespoon tomato paste

1 pound ground beef short rib

1 pound ground New York strip

2 teaspoons garlic powder

1 teaspoon smoked paprika

1 teaspoon kosher salt

1 teaspoon freshly ground black pepper

3 tablespoons minced onion

2 tablespoons finely chopped fresh flat-leaf parsley

1 pound bacon slices, halved crosswise

2 large red onions, sliced

Vegetable oil, for brushing the grill

12 slices provolone cheese

6 sesame seed buns

(continued)

To make the barbecue sauce: Place a medium pot over medium heat and add the bacon drippings and oil. When the fat is hot, add the onion and season with salt and pepper. Cook and stir for 2 minutes, or until the onion softens. Add the garlic and jalapeño and cook, stirring, for 5 minutes, or until tender. Sprinkle in the sugar, stirring to coat the vegetables. Once the sugar is incorporated, mix in the chipotle. Pour in the broth and vinegar and bring to a boil. Stir in the ketchup and tomato paste. Reduce the heat to low. Simmer, stirring occasionally, for 10 to 15 minutes, or until the sauce is thick and the color has deepened.

To make the burgers: In a small bowl, soak the bread crumbs in the beef broth and set aside to allow the bread crumbs to absorb the broth. It should look like wet sand.

In another small bowl, whisk together the egg and tomato paste until fully incorporated. Set aside.

In a large mixing bowl, combine the ground meats. Add the egg mixture and bread crumbs. Sprinkle in the garlic powder, paprika, salt, and pepper. Mix gently by hand to combine, being careful not to overwork the meat or else the burgers will be tough. Fold in the minced onion and parsley. Gently hand-form the ground beef into 6 burgers. Don't pack the meat too tightly. Set the meat aside in the refrigerator.

Put a large skillet over medium-low heat. Fry the bacon in batches for 8 minutes, or until crisp. Remove the bacon to a plate lined with paper towels. Tip out all but 3 tablespoons of the bacon fat. To the bacon drippings, add the red onions. Cook for 10 to 15 minutes, or until the onions are caramelized.

Grease a large grill pan with oil and place on two burners over medium-high heat. Or brush oil on a gas or charcoal grill to create a nonstick surface and preheat the grill to get it very hot. Grill the burgers for 4 minutes per side for medium, or 3 minutes if you like your meat rare. The burgers should turn easily without sticking.

When the burgers are just about cooked, put a couple of slices of cheese on top and allow to melt. Remove the burgers to a clean side plate so you have enough room to toast the buns.

Toast the hamburger buns cut side down for 1 minute.

Stack 2 bacon slices across the bottom half of the bun, and lay 2 more crisscrossing to make an ×, creating a platform of bacon. Lay down the hamburger patty, cheese side up, and top with one-sixth of the caramelized onion. Spread with 2 tablespoons of barbecue sauce and top with the other half of the bun. Serve the remaining barbecue sauce on the side for dipping.

Route 66 Slaw Burger

Recipe courtesy of the Blue Team (Jake, Lee, Tracy, Tony, Whitney)

For the Burger Challenge, the Blue Team set out to capture the spirit of the sandwich and create what Jake referred to as "an everyman's burger." Their Slaw Burger is a twist on the all-American classic: a blend of two types of beef served with a creamy-crunchy cabbage slaw piled high on top of the patty, instead of on the side.

SERVES 4, MAKES 2 QUARTS SLAW

FOR THE SLAW

1 cup mayonnaise

2 tablespoons apple cider vinegar

1 tablespoon Dijon mustard

1 tablespoon light brown sugar

Juice of ½ lemon

1 teaspoon celery seed

½ head green cabbage, shredded (6 cups)

½ head red cabbage, shredded (6 cups)

1 carrot, shredded

½ small red onion, grated

Kosher salt and freshly ground black pepper

FOR THE BURGERS

1 pound ground short loin

1 pound ground short rib

1 tablespoon dried onion flakes

2 teaspoons freshly ground black pepper, plus more for seasoning

1 teaspoon kosher salt, plus more for seasoning

1 teaspoon dry mustard

1 tablespoon soy sauce

4 cloves garlic, minced

8 slices Swiss cheese

4 sesame seed buns

Butter leaf lettuce

Sliced tomato

Red onion

Ketchup, mayonnaise, and Dijon mustard

To make the slaw: In a large mixing bowl, combine the mayonnaise, vinegar, mustard, sugar, lemon juice, and celery seed. Mix well and add the cabbage, carrot, and onion. Season with salt and pepper. Cover with plastic wrap and set aside in the refrigerator until ready to serve.

To make the burgers: In a large mixing bowl, combine the ground meats. Sprinkle in the dried onion, pepper, salt, and mustard. Add the soy sauce and garlic. Mix gently by hand to combine, being careful not to overwork the meat or else the burgers will be tough.

Gently hand-form the ground beef into 4 huge burgers. Don't pack the meat too tightly.

Season both sides of the burgers with salt and pepper.

(continued)

Grease a large grill pan with oil and place on two burners over medium-high heat. Or brush oil on a gas or charcoal grill to create a nonstick surface and preheat the grill, to get it very hot. Grill the burgers for 4 minutes on each side for medium, or 3 minutes if you like your meat rare. The burgers should turn easily without sticking.

When the burgers are just about cooked, put a couple of slices of cheese on top and let them melt. Remove the burgers to a clean side plate so you have enough room to toast the buns.

Toast the hamburger buns cut side down for 1 minute.

Place a leaf of butter lettuce on the bottom half of a bun. Lay down the hamburger patty, cheese side up, and top with ¼ cup of slaw. Finish with sliced tomato and red onion, and top with the bun. Serve the burgers with ketchup, mayonnaise, or Dijon mustard, and with additional slaw on the side.

Beef Tenderloin with Port-Plum Sauce and Shrimp with Passion Fruit Glaze

Recipe courtesy of Lee Knaz

The theme of the second Invention Test was romance. Lee had a choice of three evocative ingredients to cook with: rich, decadent chocolate; sweet, creamy burrata cheese; or sweet, juicy passion fruit. After some thinking, Lee opted for the passion fruit, saying, "I think I can make it sexy."

In his seductive version of surf-and-turf, Lee bathed sweet shrimp in passion fruit glaze and drizzled port wine and plum sauce over tender pieces of beef. Gordon praised the dish as "spot on" and "unique."

SERVES 4, MAKES ½ CUP SAUCE

5 passion fruit, halved (see Chef Ingredient: Passion Fruit, on page 192)

Zest, finely grated, and juice of 1 lemon

2 cloves garlic

1 shallot, minced

16 jumbo shrimp or large shrimp, peeled, deveined, tails and heads on (see Master the Basics: Peeling and Deveining Shrimp, on page 162)

5 tablespoons olive oil

4 (5-to-6-ounce) pieces beef tenderloin

Kosher salt and freshly ground black pepper

1 onion, chopped

1 carrot, chopped

1 celery stalk, chopped

4 sprigs fresh thyme

½ cup port wine

4 plums, peeled, pitted, and

chopped

½ cup Beef Broth (page 244), or quality store-bought

2 tablespoons plus ½ cup (1 stick) unsalted butter

½ head cauliflower, coarsely chopped (2 pounds)

2 parsnips, peeled and coarsely chopped

¾ cup heavy cream

Endive leaves, for garnish

Set a fine-mesh strainer over a measuring cup. Scrape out the pulp of the passion fruit with a spoon, and press it through the strainer to remove the seeds. You should get about ¼ cup of juice. Pour the juice into a shallow baking dish, add the lemon zest and juice, garlic, shallot, and shrimp. Toss to coat the shrimp thoroughly and set aside at room temperature to marinate for 20 to 30 minutes.

Preheat the oven to 300°F.

Coat a large pot or Dutch oven with 3 tablespoons of the oil and place over medium-high heat. Season the tenderloin with 1 teaspoon each salt and pepper. When the oil is hot, lay the meat in the pan and brown well

(continued)

for 2 minutes per side. Transfer the beef to a baking pan, cover with aluminum foil, and bake for 15 to 20 minutes for medium-rare.

To the meat drippings in the pot, add the onion, carrot, celery, and thyme. Cook over medium heat, stirring, for 5 minutes to soften. Remove the thyme to a small plate and set aside. Deglaze the pan with the port and cook for 1 minute to evaporate the alcohol. Add the plums and season with salt and pepper. Pour in the beef broth, and simmer gently for 10 minutes, or until the plums are soft and the liquid has reduced by half. Strain the sauce into another small pot and whisk in 2 tablespoons butter until melted and the sauce is glossy. Cover to keep warm.

Bring a large pot of salted water to a boil. Add the cauliflower and parsnips. Boil for 5 minutes, or until fork tender. Drain the vegetables in a colander. Transfer the cauliflower and parsnips to a blender. Add the cream, ½ cup butter, and ½ teaspoon each salt and pepper. Purée until the mixture is completely smooth and creamy. Cover to keep warm.

Coat a skillet with the remaining 2 tablespoons oil. When the oil is hot, add the shrimp along with the passion fruit marinade. Cook for 5 minutes, or until the shrimp curls and is firm and the marinade cooks down into a glaze.

To serve, place a few endive leaves on the side of plate and lay a couple of shrimp on top. Spoon a generous amount of the cauliflower-parsnip purée on one side of the plate, lay the steak on top, and drizzle with the port-plum sauce. Drizzle shrimp with the remaining passion fruit pan sauce. Lay a reserved thyme sprig across the top for garnish.

CHEF INGREDIENT:
Passion Fruit

If you aren't able to find fresh passion fruit, try substituting store-bought passion fruit juice or nectar. These are sold in supermarkets and often contain other sweeter juices such as apple and white grape, but you can reduce them and add lemon juice for a similar taste. For this recipe, pour 1 cup of store-bought juice into a small skillet or saucepan over medium heat, add about 2 tablespoons of lemon juice, and reduce the liquid by half.

Grahamburger with Melted Brie, Watercress, and Roasted Garlic Aïoli

Recipe courtesy of Graham Elliot

"I've eaten a few burgers in my time," Graham Elliot explains. "What makes a good one is not just the final product, it's the entire process. Mixing ground pork with the beef will give the burger a lighter mouth-feel. The lighter burger mixed with the sexy, velvety texture of the Brie and the crunch of the watercress makes for a really amazing experience that is very different from what you'll find at a standard backyard barbecue. The pretzel roll makes the whole bite almost too good to be true."

SERVES 4

1 pound ground sirloin

½ pound ground pork

1 teaspoon kosher salt

1 teaspoon freshly ground black pepper

1 cup apple cider vinegar

1½ cups olive oil, plus more for brushing the grill

1 large red onion, sliced into ⅛-inch-thick rounds

5 cloves garlic, peeled

½ cup mayonnaise

½ pound Brie cheese, sliced (see Chef Ingredient: Brie, on page 86)

4 pretzel rolls, halved lengthwise

1 bunch watercress, stems trimmed, well-washed

In a large mixing bowl, combine the beef and pork. Season with the salt and pepper. Mix gently by hand to combine, being careful not to over-work the meat or else the burgers will be tough. Gently hand-form the ground beef into 4 big burgers about 1-inch thick. Don't pack the meat too tightly. Refrigerate the patties until you are ready to grill.

Combine the vinegar and ½ cup of the oil in a large bowl. Add the onion, pushing the slices down into the liquid. Set aside for at least 30 minutes or up to 2 hours, to pickle.

In a small pot, combine the remaining 1 cup oil and the garlic. Place over medium-low heat. Simmer the garlic gently for 20 to 25 minutes, or until tender when pierced with a knife. Remove the garlic from the oil and strain off any excess oil. In a food processor or blender, combine the garlic and mayonnaise. Purée for 1 to 2 minutes, or until the garlic is well-incorporated and the mayonnaise is smooth. Place the aïoli in a small container and refrigerate. This may be made ahead and refrigerated for up to 5 days.

Brush a grill pan or a gas or charcoal grill with oil to create a nonstick surface. Preheat to medium-high.

Remove the onion from the vinegar and pat dry. Lay the onion on the grill and char for 3 minutes per side, being careful not to lose any of the slices in the grates when turning.

Grill the burgers for 8 minutes per side for medium. During the final 3 minutes, put a couple of slices of Brie on top of the patty to melt.

To assemble the burger, spread 1 tablespoon of roasted garlic aïoli on both halves of the pretzel rolls. Lay the burger on the bottom half of the roll, cheese side up, and top with a quarter of the onions. Put a small pile of watercress on top and then the top half of the roll.

Sexy Seared Filet over Sultry Bordelaise Sauce with Roasted Beet Salad and Passion Fruit Vinaigrette

Recipe courtesy of Jake Gandolfo

When Gordon Ramsay told the contestants, "This dish has to ooze romance," Jake wasn't intimidated. "I put love in my cooking. There's nothing sexier than a perfectly seared piece of meat in a blood red wine sauce." Jake continued his romantic (and red) theme with a beautiful beet salad dressed with passion fruit vinaigrette. How much sexier does it get?

1 pound beets, tops trimmed, scrubbed

9 tablespoons olive oil

Kosher salt and freshly ground black pepper

2 navel oranges, cut into segments (see Master the Basics: Segmenting Citrus, on page 53)

1 large fennel bulb, halved, cored, and thinly sliced

5 passion fruit, halved (see Master Ingredients: Passion Fruit, on page 192)

1 tablespoon red wine vinegar

4 (5-to-6-ounce) pieces filet mignon

1 shallot, minced

4 sprigs fresh oregano, leaves stripped from the stem and chopped

¼ teaspoon whole black peppercorns

1 bay leaf

1 cup dry red wine, such as Cabernet Sauvignon

1 cup store-bought or homemade demi-glace (see directions in Beef Broth recipe on page 244)

1 cup Beef Broth (page 244), or quality store-bought

2 tablespoons unsalted butter

Preheat the oven to 400°F.

Place the beets in a bowl, drizzle with 2 tablespoons of the oil, season generously with salt and pepper, and toss to coat. Lay out 2 pieces of aluminum foil, divide the beets in half, and wrap them in foil pouches, pinching to seal. Put the pouches on a baking pan and roast for 30 to 40 minutes, or until a knife pierces the beets easily without resistance. Carefully unwrap the beets and set aside to cool. When cool enough to handle, rub off the skins with paper towels. Halve the beets lengthwise and slice them into half-moons. Put the beets in a salad bowl and add the oranges and fennel.

For the vinaigrette, set a fine-mesh strainer over a measuring cup. Scrape out the pulp of the passion fruit with a spoon, and press it through the strainer to remove the seeds. You should get about ¼ cup of juice. Whisk in the vinegar and 4 tablespoons of the oil. Season with salt and pepper. Pour the vinaigrette over the beet salad and toss to coat. Taste and adjust seasoning as needed. Set aside in the refrigerator to allow the flavors to come together.

Coat a large pot or Dutch oven with the remaining 3 tablespoons oil over medium-high heat. Season the filet mignon with 1 teaspoon each salt and pepper. When the oil is hot, lay the meat in the pan and brown well, for 4 minutes per side. Remove the meat from the pan and set aside on a cutting board to rest, covered, for 10 minutes.

To the meat drippings in the pot, add the shallot, oregano, peppercorns, and bay leaf. Cook over medium heat, stirring, for 1 minute to soften the shallot. Deglaze the pan with the wine and cook for 1 minute to evaporate the alcohol. Stir in the demi-glace and broth and simmer gently for 10 minutes, or until the liquid has reduced by half. Strain the sauce into another small pot and whisk in the butter until melted and the sauce is glossy. Cover to keep warm.

To serve, cut the steak on the bias into ½-inch-thick slices. Layer the meat in an overlapping pattern on each plate, drizzle with the bordelaise sauce, and serve the beet salad on the side.

Pan-Roasted Venison Tenderloin with Red Wine–Blueberry Reduction over Creamed Brussels Sprouts

Recipe courtesy of Sheetal Bhagat

For the final Mystery Box Challenge, the six contestants were given one hour to create a stunning dish using venison. Wild game tends to be very lean and, consequently, can be tough and dry if not cooked properly. None of the contestants had much experience cooking venison, and Sheetal, who doesn't eat meat, had never worked with venison before. So she was surprised—and elated—when the compliments started flowing for her pan-roasted venison tenderloin, which Joe lauded as "restaurant quality."

SERVES 4

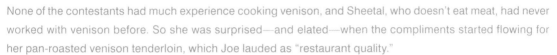

4 bacon strips

4 (5-to-6-ounce) venison tenderloin steaks (about 2 inches thick and 4 inches long), patted dry

Kosher salt and freshly ground black pepper

¼ cup olive oil

8 sprigs fresh thyme

3 cloves garlic, crushed

2 shallots, minced

¾ cup dry red wine, such as Cabernet Sauvignon

½ cup Beef Broth (page 244), or quality store-bought

1 cup fresh blueberries, mashed

1 tablespoon sugar

1 pound Brussels sprouts, blanched (see Master the Basics: Blanching, on page 132)

2 tablespoons unsalted butter

¼ cup heavy cream

Pinch of freshly grated nutmeg

Preheat the oven to 350°F.

Wrap a piece of bacon around the center of each piece of tenderloin and secure with a toothpick. Season with 1 teaspoon each salt and pepper. Pour 3 tablespoons of the oil in a large ovenproof skillet over medium heat. Add 2 thyme sprigs and 2 crushed garlic cloves and cook for 1 minute, or until fragrant. Lay the meat in the skillet and sear for 2 to 3 minutes per side, or until the bacon is crispy.

Transfer the skillet to the oven and finish cooking for 7 minutes, for medium-rare (135° to 140°F). Remove and let rest for 15 minutes, covered with aluminum foil to keep the meat warm and moist.

Meanwhile, heat the remaining 1 tablespoon oil in a pot over medium heat. Add half of the shallots and the remaining thyme and garlic. Season with salt and pepper, and sweat for about 30 seconds. Pour in the wine and

broth. Bring to a boil, then lower the heat and cook for 7 minutes, reducing the liquid by half. Add the mashed blueberries (juice and pulp) and sugar. Season with salt and pepper. Stir the blueberries gently, and cook on medium-low heat for 10 minutes. Pass the blueberry sauce through a fine-mesh strainer and set aside.

Slice the Brussels sprouts about ⅛ inch thick. Melt the butter in a skillet over medium heat. Add the remaining shallots, season with salt and pepper, and sweat for about 1 minute. Add the Brussels sprouts and cook for 2 minutes, tossing to coat and get some color. Pour in the cream and add the nutmeg. Simmer for 5 minutes, adjusting the seasoning at the end.

To serve, cut the venison into ¼-inch-thick slices. Place a pile of Brussels sprouts in the middle of the plate and crumble the bacon bits around. Fan the sliced venison over the Brussels sprouts and spoon the sauce on top.

Veal Saltimbocca with Oven-Roasted Roma Tomatoes

Recipe courtesy of Tony Carbone

For his signature dish, the Italian from Boston cooked his rendition of the classic Roman dish, Veal Saltimbocca, for the judges. Literally translated as "jumps in the mouth," saltimbocca bursts with the flavor of veal, sage, prosciutto, and butter. Tony turned tradition on its ear by including smoked mozzarella in his recipe. The judges agreed he had potential and welcomed him to the competition.

SERVES 4

FOR THE TOMATOES

4 plum (Roma) tomatoes, halved lengthwise

2 tablespoons extra-virgin olive oil

1 tablespoon balsamic vinegar

2 cloves garlic, minced

2 sprigs fresh thyme

Kosher salt and freshly ground black pepper

FOR THE VEAL

4 (5-ounce) thinly sliced veal cutlets (scallopini)

4 ounces thinly sliced prosciutto

1 (4-ounce) block smoked mozzarella, cut into 4 slices

8 fresh sage leaves, plus more for garnish

½ cup all-purpose flour

Kosher salt and freshly ground black pepper

2 tablespoons extra-virgin olive oil, plus more for serving

2 tablespoons unsalted butter

2 tablespoons dry white wine, such as Pinot Grigio

¼ cup Chicken Broth (page 242), or quality store-bought

Angel hair pasta, cooked al dente (see Master the Basics: Cooking Pasta, on page 96)

Lemon wedges

To make the tomatoes: Preheat the oven to 400°F.

Put the tomatoes in a large bowl. Drizzle with oil and vinegar. Toss in the garlic and thyme and season with salt and pepper. Toss the tomatoes to coat in the flavored oil. Arrange the tomatoes on a baking pan in a single layer, cut side up. Pour any remaining oil from the bowl over the tomatoes and bake for 30 to 40 minutes to concentrate their flavor. They should be shrunken and dry to the touch.

To make the veal: Put the veal cutlets side by side on a sheet of plastic wrap. Lay a piece of prosciutto on top of each piece of veal, followed by a slice of mozzarella on each, and cover with another piece of plastic.

(continued)

Gently flatten the cutlets with a rolling pin or meat mallet, until the pieces are about ¼ inch thick and the ham and cheese have adhered to the veal.

Remove the plastic and lay a couple of sage leaves in the center of each cutlet. Roll the veal away from you into a log. Weave a toothpick or skewer in and out of the veal to secure the filling. Spread the flour out on a shallow platter and season with a fair amount of salt and pepper. Mix with a fork to combine. Dredge the veal in the seasoned flour, shaking off the excess.

Heat the oil and 1 tablespoon of butter in a large skillet over medium heat. When the butter has melted, lay the veal in the pan, and cook for 3 minutes, or until it forms a crispy crust. Using tongs, carefully flip the veal over to cook the other side for 2 minutes, or until golden. Transfer the saltimbocca to a serving platter, remove the toothpicks, and keep warm.

Pour the wine into the same skillet, stirring with a wooden spoon to bring up all the flavor from the bottom. Let the wine cook down for a minute to burn off some of the alcohol. Add the broth and the remaining 1 tablespoon butter and swirl the pan around. Season with salt and pepper.

To serve, arrange a serving of pasta on each plate and drizzle with olive oil. Lay a veal cutlet on top, pour the sauce on top, and garnish with the loose cooked sage leaves and lemon wedges. Place the tomatoes on the side.

Thick-Cut Veal Milanese with Arugula Salad

Recipe courtesy of Dave Miller

As part of a Head-to-Head challenge, judge Joe Bastianich asked the contestants to make him a stunning Veal Milanese. Dave created his own distinct take on the northern Italian classic and used meaty, marbled, bone-in veal chops instead of typical thin veal cutlets. Dave says, "I wanted to give the judges 'man-food.'"

SERVES 4

4 (8-to-10-ounce) bone-in veal chops

Kosher salt and freshly ground black pepper

1 cup all-purpose flour

2 large eggs

1 tablespoon heavy cream

1 cup plain dried bread crumbs

2 tablespoons freshly grated Parmesan cheese

2 teaspoons dried oregano

2 teaspoons dried basil

5 tablespoons olive oil

2 cups grape tomatoes, halved lengthwise

4 cups baby arugula, loosely packed

Finely grated zest and juice of 1 lemon, plus wedges for garnish

Preheat the oven to 350°F.

Pound the veal chops between two sheets of plastic wrap with a mallet or heavy skillet to ¼-inch thickness. Season the chops on both sides generously with salt and pepper.

Set up an assembly line: Spread the flour out in a shallow dish and season with salt and pepper. In another bowl, whisk the eggs and cream and beat to combine. In another shallow dish or bowl, mix the bread crumbs, cheese, and dried herbs and season with ¼ teaspoon each salt and pepper.

Lightly dredge both sides of the veal in the seasoned flour. Dip each chop into the egg wash, allowing the excess to drip back into the bowl. Finish by rolling it in the bread crumb mixture, coating evenly and gently pressing the crumbs so they adhere to the meat. Set the chops on a large plate.

Coat an ovenproof or cast-iron skillet with 3 tablespoons of the oil and place over medium heat. When the oil is hot, lay the chops in the pan, working in batches if necessary, and cook for 2 to 3 minutes per side, or until nicely browned, taking care not to burn the bread crumbs. Transfer the pan to the oven and finish cooking for 6 to 8 minutes, or until medium-rare. Remove the veal chops to a cutting board and let rest for 5 minutes so the juices settle back into the meat.

Meanwhile, combine the tomatoes, arugula, lemon zest and juice, and the remaining 2 tablespoons oil in a bowl. Season with salt and pepper. Toss gently to coat.

To serve, lay a veal chop in the center of each plate and top with a pile of the arugula salad. Garnish with lemon wedges.

Herb and Panko-Crusted Rack of Lamb with Fennel Risotto

Recipe courtesy of Lee Knaz

Lee grew up in Israel and has a fondness for the big flavors of the Mediterranean. After serving time in the Israeli army, Lee packed his bags and moved to Los Angeles to cultivate his passion for healthy cuisine. For his signature dish, he created a perfectly cooked rack of lamb with a Mediterranean-influenced fennel risotto. Gordon praised the quality of Lee's lamb, admitting that "many professional chefs can't cook lamb precisely medium-rare." For once, the three judges could agree on something: Lee's dish was one of the best, worthy enough to secure him a spot in the next round.

SERVES 4 TO 6

FOR THE LAMB

1 cup panko (Japanese) bread crumbs

1 tablespoon finely chopped fresh sage leaves

2 teaspoons finely chopped fresh rosemary leaves

2 tablespoons finely chopped fresh mint leaves, plus more for garnish

1 teaspoon red-pepper flakes

Kosher salt and freshly ground black pepper

4 tablespoons extra-virgin olive oil

2 (6-rib) Frenched racks of lamb (1½ pounds each), trimmed of all but a thin layer of fat, rinsed and patted dry (see Chef Ingredient: Rack of Lamb, on page 184)

3 tablespoons Dijon mustard

FOR THE RISOTTO

6 cups Chicken Broth (page 242), or quality store-bought

2 whole star anise

1 teaspoon coriander seeds

2 tablespoons extra-virgin olive oil

1 small onion, finely diced

1 fennel bulb, halved, cored, and sliced

1 cup Arborio or carnaroli rice

Kosher salt and freshly ground black pepper

1 cup dry white wine, such as Pinot Grigio

1 tablespoon unsalted butter

1 cup grated Parmesan cheese

To make the lamb: Preheat the oven to 375°F.

In a wide shallow dish, combine the bread crumbs, sage, rosemary, mint, and red-pepper flakes. Season with 1 teaspoon salt and ½ teaspoon pepper. Drizzle in 2 tablespoons of the oil and rub the bread crumb mixture with your fingers to evenly moisten. Set aside.

(continued)

Season the lamb on all sides with a generous amount of salt and pepper. You should see the seasoning on the meat. Coat a large, wide ovenproof skillet with the remaining 2 tablespoons oil and place over medium-high heat. Lay the lamb racks in the hot oil, fat side down. Sear on all sides, turning with tongs, for 3 minutes, or until well-browned. Carefully remove the lamb from the skillet and brush the mustard all over the meat. Dredge the lamb in the bread crumb mixture, being sure to coat evenly.

Return the lamb to the skillet and transfer to the oven. Bake for 15 to 20 minutes, or until the internal temperature of the lamb reads 130°F when an instant read thermometer is inserted into the meat. Remove the lamb from the oven, cover with aluminum foil, and let rest before cutting into the chops.

To make the risotto: In a medium pot, combine the broth, star anise, and coriander over medium-low heat and keep warm.

Coat a large, deep skillet with the oil and place over medium heat. When the oil is hot, add the onion and fennel. Cook, stirring, for 4 minutes, or until the vegetables are soft. Add the rice and stir for 1 or 2 minutes, or until well-coated. Season with salt and pepper. Stir in the wine and simmer for 1 minute to evaporate the alcohol.

Pour in 1 cup of the warm broth. Stir with a wooden spoon until the rice has absorbed all of the liquid. Keep stirring while adding the broth little by little, allowing the rice to absorb the liquid before adding more. Cook for 20 minutes, or until the rice is tender but slightly firm to the bite. Remove from the heat and stir in the butter and cheese.

To serve, divide the risotto among 4 plates, top with a lamb chop, and garnish with mint.

CHEF INGREDIENTS:

Rack of Lamb

Rack of lamb, sold whole with 6 to 8 ribs, is undoubtedly the most prized cut of lamb. The meat on the rack is exceptionally tender and has a fine flavor. Rack of lamb is often Frenched, meaning the rib bones are cleaned of meat and connective tissue before cooking to create an elegant presentation. Rack of lamb is easy to carve, and at its best it is simply roasted and served medium-rare.

Risotto

Risotto, a traditional Italian rice dish cooked with broth, is typically made with a type of short-grained Italian rice called Arborio rice, which is widely available at most supermarkets. Another excellent choice is carnaroli rice, a medium-grained Italian rice with a higher starch content that lends a firmer texture to the risotto.

DESSERTS

Banana Pudding "Napoleon"

Recipe courtesy of Tracy Nailor

For the Egg Challenge, Tracy went out on a limb and prepared a dessert. As she was the only contestant to create a sweet dish, Graham Elliot called the move "gutsy." For Tracy, banana pudding is a comfort food— a classic recipe from her childhood. She has fond memories of helping her mother make this simple, yet special dessert. "The flavors of sweet banana and creamy vanilla custard bring me back to being a little girl standing on a step stool to help my mother whisk," she says.

SERVES 2

2 tablespoons unsalted butter

2 ripe bananas, sliced

7 tablespoons sugar

1 large egg, separated (see Master the Basics: Separating an Egg on the opposite page)

1 tablespoon all-purpose flour

½ cup whole milk

1 vanilla bean, split and scraped

2 (8-inch) flour tortillas

Put a small skillet over medium heat and add the butter. When the butter gets foamy, add the banana. Sprinkle with 1 tablespoon of the sugar. Cook and stir for 3 to 4 minutes, or until the bananas have caramelized and softened. Set aside.

Put the egg white in a clean glass or metal bowl. Using a handheld electric mixer or whisk, beat vigorously until the egg white foams and begins to thicken into soft peaks. Sprinkle in 2 tablespoons of the sugar. Continue beating until the meringue forms peaks with tips that stand straight when the beaters are lifted. Set aside.

Fill a pot halfway with water and bring to a simmer over medium heat. Combine the flour and 2 tablespoons of the sugar in a heatproof bowl. Put the bowl over the pot of simmering water, making sure the bottom does not touch the water. Slowly whisk in the milk and egg yolk. Scrape the vanilla bean into the pot and add the pod for extra flavor. Cook, whisking often, for 5 to 7 minutes, or until the mixture becomes a thick custard.

Place a dry skillet over high heat. Lay a tortilla in the pan and sprinkle with ½ tablespoon of the sugar. Cook for 2 minutes, or until the bottom of the tortilla is lightly golden. Flip the tortilla over and sprinkle with the remaining ½ tablespoon sugar. Repeat with the second tortilla.

To assemble, lay a tortilla on a plate. Discard the vanilla bean and pour half of the custard on top of the tortilla. Scatter with half of the sautéed bananas. Repeat the three layers. Top with the meringue and use a spoon to form decorative peaks. Using a blowtorch, brown the meringue, if desired.

MASTER THE BASICS:

SEPARATING AN EGG

To separate an egg, crack the egg and hold the shell halves over a bowl. Transfer the yolk back and forth between the halves, letting the white drop into the bowl. Do not cut the yolk—if egg whites contain even a smidgen of the yolk, they won't form stiff peaks when beaten. Transfer the yolk to another bowl, and, if not using immediately, cover and store it in the fridge for up to a few days and use it in a yolk-heavy recipe, such as custard.

Brandy-Infused Chocolate Mousse with Candied Lemon Peel

Recipe courtesy of Sheena Zadeh

For the initial Mystery Box Challenge, the 14 finalists found a box of mostly savory ingredients, with a few surprises thrown in—including chocolate. Judge Joe Bastianich warned, "Chocolate is the devil in the box. It will tempt you and take you down the wrong path if you are not careful." Going against the grain, Sheena decided to make a chocolate mousse. She recalls, "Chocolate, cream, eggs, and sugar jumped out at me. It was like a chocolate mousse waiting to happen. I wanted to think outside the box literally and figuratively." Sheena says she felt excited and validated when she learned that her chocolate mousse was one of the judges' favorite dishes.

SERVES 6

1 lemon

1 cup sugar

2 cups heavy cream

2 large egg yolks

1 tablespoon brandy

6 ounces quality bittersweet
chocolate, chopped
(about 1 cup)

To candy the lemon peel, use a vegetable peeler to remove the peel from the lemon in vertical strips. Try to remove only the yellow zest, avoiding as much of the white pith as possible. Save the lemon for another use.

Combine ½ cup of the sugar and 1 cup of water in a small pot over medium heat, whisking until the sugar dissolves. Add the lemon peels and reduce the heat to medium-low. Simmer, uncovered, for 20 minutes, or until the peels are tender and translucent.

Meanwhile, pour ¾ cup of the cream into a small pot and place over medium heat. Keep the remaining cream chilled to whip later. In a mixing bowl, whisk together the yolks, brandy, and the remaining ½ cup sugar until pale yellow. Pour in the hot cream in a slow stream, whisking until combined. Take care to add the cream slowly so the eggs do not get too hot and scramble. Pour the mixture back into the pot and gently simmer over low heat, stirring constantly, until it coats the back of a spoon. Remove from the heat.

Melt the chocolate in a microwave or in a metal bowl set over barely simmering water. Stir until the chocolate is completely smooth and shiny. Let cool slightly. Whisk the custard into the melted chocolate until smooth. Set aside in the refrigerator.

Using a handheld electric mixer in a chilled bowl, beat the remaining 1¼ cups cream until it develops stiff peaks. Fold about one-third of the whipped cream into the cooled chocolate to lighten, then fold the rest in until thoroughly combined. Some white streaks will remain. The chocolate mixture will be pourable and will set up as it chills.

Spoon the chocolate mousse into 6 individual serving dishes or glasses. Cover and refrigerate for a couple of hours.

Garnish with the candied lemon peel before serving.

Red, White, and Blue Napoleon

Recipe courtesy of the Blue Team (Mike, Jake, Tony, Lee, Tracy, Sheetal)

When the contestants were faced with the task of feeding a group of hungry Marines, the Blue Team selected Tracy to be in charge of dessert. "We wanted to make the Marines a dessert that was inspired by the most important symbol of America: the flag," she says. "For our men and women in uniform, we created a layered fruit napoleon that possessed a light, fresh taste of home. The flavors are reminiscent of a cross between strawberry shortcake and blueberry cobbler. The cream is definitely the star of this dish but does not overpower the fresh fruit." This colorful napoleon is the perfect dessert for a Fourth of July barbecue.

SERVES 12

2 tablespoons unsalted butter, melted

3 sheets (11 × 17 inches) frozen puff pastry, thawed

1 large egg

1 pint heavy cream, cold

2 tablespoons pure vanilla extract

1½ cups sugar

3 pints fresh blueberries (about 6 cups)

¼ cup light corn syrup

2 tablespoons fresh lemon juice

2 pints strawberries, hulled and thinly sliced (about 3 cups)

Preheat the oven to 350°F.

Brush 3 baking pans with the melted butter and lay a sheet of puff pastry onto each. Whisk the egg and 1 tablespoon of water in a small bowl. Brush the egg wash on the surface of the pastry sheets in a light, even layer. Bake for 15 minutes, or until the pastry is golden brown.

Pour the cream into a bowl and beat with a handheld electric mixer on low speed until it begins to foam and thicken. Add 1 tablespoon of the vanilla and beat to incorporate. Gradually sprinkle in 1 cup of the sugar. Increase the speed to medium and continue to beat until the cream holds stiff peaks, taking care not to overwhip. Cover and chill.

Combine 2 pints of the blueberries and the remaining ½ cup sugar with ½ cup of water in a medium pot over medium heat. Cook for 5 minutes, or until the berries start to get plump. Add the corn syrup, lemon juice, and the remaining 1 tablespoon vanilla. Let simmer for 15 minutes, or until the berries begin to burst and the liquid is reduced to the consistency of syrup. Set the blueberry compote aside to cool at room temperature.

To assemble, place a sheet of puff pastry on a serving platter. Spoon one-third of the blueberry compote over the pastry. Spoon a generous layer of cream (about 1 cup) on top of the compote. Top with a layer of fresh blueberries and strawberries. Repeat two more times, ending with a top layer of fresh berries. Serve with a dollop of whipped cream in the middle of each portion.

Hazelnut and Pistachio Cupcake with Hazelnut Cream Cheese Icing

Recipe courtesy of Sharone Hakman

One Mystery Box Challenge stands out as the sweetest of them all. After the contestants lifted the lids off of their boxes to find a muffin pan, milk, eggs, flour, sugar, butter, and vanilla, the judges announced what most of the contestants already suspected: It was cupcake time!

They were also given an array of ingredients to create their own signature cupcake, from chocolate and sprinkles to fruit and nuts. One ingredient, in particular, stood out to Sharone, who admits, "I've never attempted to bake cupcakes in my life. That's my wife's specialty. I wanted to create an homage to Nutella, one of the most delicious things on the planet." After tasting his unique, whimsical treat, Joe exclaimed, "It has a Willy Wonka thing to it. Exquisitely decorated, it looks as amazing as it tastes!"

MAKES 12

FOR THE BATTER

3 cups all-purpose flour

1 tablespoon baking powder

½ teaspoon kosher salt

⅔ cup unsalted butter, at room temperature

½ cup dark chocolate chips, melted

½ cup milk chocolate chips, melted

1½ cups granulated sugar

1½ teaspoons pure vanilla extract

½ cup shelled pistachios, toasted

½ cup shelled hazelnuts, toasted

2 large eggs

1¼ cups whole milk

1 tablespoon chocolate-hazelnut spread

FOR THE FROSTING

2 packages (8 ounces) cream cheese, at room temperature

4 cups confectioners' sugar

1 tablespoon chocolate-hazelnut spread, softened

To make the batter: Preheat the oven to 350°F. Line a standard 12-cup muffin pan with silicone cups or liners coated with vegetable cooking spray.

Sift together the flour, baking powder, and salt in a bowl. Set aside.

Using a handheld or standing electric mixer, whip the butter for 1 minute, or until creamy and fluffy. Add the melted chocolate chips and continue to beat until combined, scraping down the sides of the bowl with a rubber spatula. Add the sugar and vanilla and beat for 4 minutes, or until the sugar is fully incorporated and the mixture is light.

Chop 2 tablespoons each of the pistachios and hazelnuts and mix them into the batter. Add the eggs, one at a time, beating well between additions and continuing to scrape the bowl. Add the dry ingredients, alternating with the milk, beating well until smooth. Using a rubber spatula, swirl in the hazelnut spread by hand.

Divide the batter evenly in the cupcake pan. Bake for 22 to 25 minutes, or until the cupcakes spring back when touched gently in the center. Remove from the oven and cool completely before decorating. If you have difficulty unmolding the cupcakes, run a small icing spatula or a thin knife around the perimeter of each cupcake.

To make the frosting: Using a handheld electric mixer, beat the cream cheese until whipped and light. Gradually sprinkle in the confectioners' sugar and continue to beat until thick. Fold in the hazelnut spread using a small spatula or spoon, or a wooden skewer for a finer swirl.

To assemble, spoon the frosting into a piping bag and squeeze it onto the cooled cupcakes. Top with the reserved whole nuts.

Chocolate Lover's Cupcake with Raspberry Coulis

Recipe courtesy of Jake Gandolfo

Jake chose a classic combination for his signature cupcake: rich chocolate cake mellowed by the sweet-tart flavor of raspberries. Jake's super-chocolatey dessert surprised Gordon, who compared Jake to a bull in a china shop and asked, "How can you cook with such finesse?" Joe agreed, commenting, "The texture is so light, like a perfect flourless chocolate cake. It transcends the quality of what a cupcake would be. If you're trying to fool us, we're onto you, Jake!"

MAKES 12

FOR THE BATTER

1 cup boiling water

½ cup cocoa powder

¼ cup whole milk

3 cups all-purpose flour

1 tablespoon baking powder

½ teaspoon kosher salt

⅔ cup unsalted butter, at room temperature

1½ cups granulated sugar

1½ teaspoons pure vanilla extract

2 large eggs

FOR THE FROSTING

½ cup (1 stick) unsalted butter, at room temperature

1 teaspoon pure vanilla extract

2 cups confectioners' sugar, plus more for dusting the plate

1 cup cocoa powder

¼ cup whole milk

FOR THE COULIS

1 pint fresh raspberries, reserving 12 for garnish

3 tablespoons light brown sugar

3 tablespoons orange liqueur, such as Grand Marnier

FOR THE GANACHE

6 ounces bittersweet chocolate, coarsely chopped (about 1 cup)

¼ cup heavy cream

2 tablespoons unsalted butter

Pinch of salt

½ cup chopped macadamia nuts

To make the batter: Preheat the oven to 350°F. Line a standard 12-cup muffin pan with silicone cups or liners coated with vegetable cooking spray.

Whisk the boiling water into a small bowl of cocoa powder until it becomes a smooth liquid. Pour in the milk, continuing to whisk until well incorporated. Set aside.

Sift together the flour, baking powder, and salt in a bowl. Set aside.

Using a handheld or standing electric mixer, whip the butter, sugar, and vanilla in a large mixing bowl until light and creamy. Add the eggs, one at a time, beating well between additions and scraping down the sides

(continued)

of the bowl with a rubber spatula. Add the dry ingredients, alternating with the cocoa mixture, starting with the mixer on low to prevent splatter and gradually increasing the speed until the cocoa is fully incorporated and the batter is smooth.

Divide the batter evenly in the cupcake pan. Bake for 20 to 22 minutes, or until the cupcakes spring back when touched gently in the center. Remove from the oven and cool completely before decorating.

To make the frosting: Using a handheld electric mixer, beat the butter and vanilla until whipped and light. Gradually sprinkle in the confectioners' sugar and cocoa powder and continue to beat until thick (the batter may appear grainy or lumpy, but adding the milk will smooth it out). Pour in the milk very gradually and continue beating until well combined and the frosting is smooth and spreadable.

To make the coulis: Combine the raspberries, brown sugar, orange liqueur, and 2 tablespoons of water in a pot over medium heat. Cook for 7 to 10 minutes, or until the berries start to break down and form a sauce. Set a fine-mesh strainer over a bowl or measuring cup. Press the raspberry mixture through the strainer to remove the seeds. Set the coulis aside to cool.

To make the ganache: Melt the chocolate in a microwave or in a metal bowl set over barely simmering water. Stir until the chocolate is completely smooth and shiny. Let it cool slightly. In a microwave-safe bowl, heat the heavy cream just until warmed, about 30 seconds. In very small increments, stir in the warmed cream—if you add too much cream at once, the ganache can "break." It may stiffen slightly, but continue to stir and add the cream gradually. Gently fold in the butter and salt and continue to mix until the ganache becomes silky and shiny.

Unmold the cooled cupcakes. Using an offset spatula and rotating the cupcake in a circular motion, cover the top of the cupcake with frosting in smooth strokes, taking care not to press into the cupcake.

To serve, sift confectioners' sugar over the serving plate and place a cupcake on one side. With the tip of a small metal spoon or a squeeze bottle, paint a stroke of coulis and a stroke of ganache on the plate beside the cupcake. Top the ganache with about a teaspoon of chopped macadamia nuts and the reserved raspberries.

Variation: If you're a real chocolate purist, simply pour the ganache over the top of each cupcake. Top each one with a raspberry.

Faruq

Raspberry Red Velvet Cupcake

Recipe courtesy of Faruq Jenkins

"I was devastated when the judges told me they didn't think this cupcake was my best offering," says Faruq. "I really took their advice to heart and worked on the recipe until it was perfect!" The result? A cupcake that's moist, rich, and ever so slightly tangy (thanks to the sour cream frosting). These pretty cupcakes boast a stunning red interior and are the perfect treat for Christmas or Valentine's Day dessert tables.

MAKES 12

FOR THE BATTER

3¾ cups cake flour

¼ cup cocoa powder

1 tablespoon baking powder

½ teaspoon kosher salt

⅔ cup unsalted butter, at room temperature

1½ cups granulated sugar

2 tablespoons red food coloring

1 tablespoon pure vanilla extract

2 large eggs

1¼ cups whole milk

FOR THE FROSTING

½ cup (1 stick) unsalted butter, at room temperature

1 teaspoon pure vanilla extract

2 cups confectioners' sugar, sifted

2 tablespoons heavy cream

2 tablespoons sour cream

½ cup raspberries, slightly mashed with a fork

Sprinkles, for garnish

To make the batter: Preheat the oven to 350°F. Line a standard 12-cup muffin pan with silicone cups or liners coated with vegetable cooking spray.

Sift together the flour, cocoa powder, baking powder, and salt in a bowl. Set aside.

Using a handheld or standing electric mixer, whip the butter, sugar, food coloring, and vanilla until light and creamy, scraping down the sides of the bowl with a rubber spatula. Add the eggs, one at a time, beating well between additions. Add the dry ingredients, alternating with the milk, beating well until smooth and continuing to scrape the bowl.

Divide the batter evenly in the cupcake pan. Bake for 18 to 20 minutes, or until the cupcakes spring back when touched gently in the center. Remove from the oven and cool completely before decorating.

To make the frosting: Using a handheld electric mixer, beat the butter and vanilla until whipped and light. Gradually sprinkle in the confectioner's sugar and continue beating until thick. Add the heavy cream and sour cream and beat until well incorporated. Gently fold in the raspberries.

Spoon the frosting into a piping bag and pipe on top of the cooled cupcakes. Top with red or other sprinkles.

Profiteroles with Vanilla Chantilly Cream and Caramelized Bananas

Recipe courtesy of Whitney Miller

"My inspiration for the dessert came from my love for the Southern classic, flambéed bananas foster with vanilla ice cream," Whitney shares. "In the craziness of the competition, I accidentally burnt my first batch of profiteroles, so I needed to start over. It was worth it because they came out perfectly the second time around."

After tasting this uniquely delicious version of bananas foster, the judges declared it the hands-down winner.

SERVES 4, MAKES 20

½ cup all-purpose flour

½ teaspoon plus 2 cups plus 2 tablespoons granulated sugar

¼ teaspoon salt

½ cup (1 stick) unsalted butter

2 large eggs

2 cups heavy cream, cold

1 vanilla bean, split and scraped

¾ cup confectioners' sugar, plus more for garnish

3 bananas, sliced ¼ inch thick on a bias

2 tablespoons brandy

Preheat the oven to 400°F. Line two baking pans with parchment paper or Silpat.

In a small bowl, sift the flour, ½ teaspoon granulated sugar, and salt. Set aside.

In a medium pot, combine ¼ cup of the butter and ½ cup of water. Bring to a boil over high heat. Add the dry ingredients and stir constantly with a wooden spoon for 2 minutes, or until the mixture pulls away from the side of the pot. Remove from the heat and whisk in the eggs for 2 minutes, or until incorporated and the mixture comes together to form a ball of dough.

Scoop the dough into a pastry bag fitted with a large plain round tip or into a plastic storage bag with a hole about the size of a dime cut in one corner. Pipe about 20 golf ball–size mounds onto the prepared baking pans. Dip your finger in water and lightly smooth out the peaks of all the puffs. Bake for 25 to 30 minutes, or until golden brown. Remove the profiteroles from the pan and set aside to cool. Wipe off the Silpat or replace the parchment—you'll need this for the caramel.

Beat the cream with a handheld electric mixer until it forms soft peaks. Add the vanilla seeds and sift in the confectioners' sugar, folding it into

(continued)

the cream. Scoop the whipped cream into a pastry bag fitted with a plain round tip. Refrigerate until ready to use.

In a small pot over medium heat, combine the 2 cups granulated sugar with ¾ cup of water. It should look like wet sand. Swirl the pot over the burner to dissolve the sugar completely. Cook for 5 minutes, or until the sugar melts and begins to turn golden. Continue to cook 3 minutes longer, or until the color deepens to medium amber. Be careful, the sugar is really hot at this point. Remove from the heat. Pour the hot caramel onto the prepared baking pan. Let it cool and harden for 15 minutes and then break up into long shards.

Melt the remaining ¼ cup butter in a skillet over medium heat. When the butter gets foamy, add the bananas and sprinkle with 2 tablespoons granulated sugar. Cook and stir for 3 minutes, or until the bananas have caramelized on one side and the sugar has melted. Flip the bananas and remove the pan from the heat. Pour in the brandy and ignite with a gas burner flame or long kitchen lighter. Toss the bananas and cook 2 minutes longer.

Make a hole in the bottom of each profiterole and pipe the vanilla cream inside.

To assemble, put 5 banana slices on a plate in a circle. Top each banana slice with a profiterole, letting the outer end of the banana show. Place 3 pieces of your caramel design in the center of each profiterole ring. Dust with confectioners' sugar.

Vanilla Crème Brulee with Vanilla, Orange, and Mango Coulis

Recipe courtesy of Dave Miller

After securing a win with her venison dish, Sheetal had the advantage of choosing the next Mystery Box ingredient. Faced with an array of honey, berries, and vanilla products (including beans, extract, and syrup), Sheetal chose stunning vanilla pods. Dave, who says he loves to order crème brulee in restaurants, was immediately inspired to make a tropical version of his favorite dessert. The judges praised the contrasting flavors of sweet tropical fruits and bitter orange.

SERVES 6

6 large egg yolks

½ cup plus 3 tablespoons sugar

1 quart heavy cream

2 vanilla beans

2 oranges, 1 thinly sliced and 1 juiced

2 lemons, 1 thinly sliced and 1 juiced

1 tablespoon orange liqueur, such as Grand Marnier

1 ripe mango, halved, seeded, and diced (see Master the Basics: Cubing a Mango, on page 46)

Preheat the oven to 325°F.

In a large bowl, cream together the egg yolks and ½ cup sugar with a whisk until the mixture is pale yellow and thick.

Pour the cream into a medium pot over low heat. Using a paring knife, split 1 vanilla bean down the middle, scrape out the seeds, and add them to the pot, discarding the pod. Bring the cream to a brief simmer—do not boil or it will overflow. Remove from the heat and temper the yolks by gradually whisking the hot vanilla cream into the yolk and sugar mixture. Take care not to add the hot cream too quickly or the eggs can scramble.

Divide the custard among six (6-ounce) ramekins or crème brulee dishes. Place the ramekins in a roasting pan and fill the pan with enough hot water to come halfway up the sides of the ramekins. Bake for 40 minutes, or until barely set around the edges. Remove from the oven and cool to room temperature. Transfer the ramekins to the refrigerator and chill for at least 2 hours or up to overnight.

Using a paring knife, split the remaining vanilla bean down the middle, scrape out the seeds, and add to a pot along with the pods. Add the orange and lemon juices, orange liqueur, and 2 tablespoons of the sugar. Cook over medium heat for 5 minutes, or until reduced slightly.

Add the mango and continue to simmer for 5 to 10 minutes, or until the juice cooks down to a syrup. Cool slightly and remove the vanilla pod.

Transfer the fruit mixture to a blender and purée until smooth. Strain it through a fine-mesh strainer into a bowl or measuring cup. Chill the coulis for at least 20 minutes.

Sprinkle the remaining 1 tablespoon sugar on top of each chilled custard. Hold a kitchen torch 2 inches above the surface to brown the sugar and form a crust. Serve with the coulis on the side. Garnish with the orange and lemon slices.

Bittersweet Chocolate Soufflés

 Recipe courtesy of MasterChef **Kitchen**

The final five contestants returned to the kitchen for a face-off between Whitney and Sharone in the last Pressure Test of the competition. Gordon set the stage with a pun: "Which one of you is going to RISE to the occasion and which one of you is going to FALL flat on your face?"

A luxurious chocolate soufflé is a grand finale to a perfect dinner. Soufflé is one of those top-level desserts that, when executed with mastery, is as impressive as it is delicious.

SERVES 6

5 tablespoons unsalted butter, plus more for greasing

¼ cup sugar, plus more for dusting

4 ounces bittersweet chocolate, coarsely chopped

3 large egg yolks

¼ cup warm water

5 large egg whites

½ teaspoon cream of tartar

Position a rack in the center of the oven and preheat to 425°F.

Prepare six (6-ounce) individual ramekins by greasing with softened butter and coating with sugar. Pour out any excess. The butter and sugar will keep the soufflés from sticking to the sides and will allow them to rise evenly. The sugar will also give the soufflé a crunchy crust, which is a great contrast to the soft interior.

Melt the chocolate and the 5 tablespoons butter in a metal bowl set over a pot of barely simmering water, stirring occasionally until smooth. Remove the bowl from the heat and set aside.

Using a standing electric mixer, beat the egg yolks and warm water in a medium bowl at high speed until doubled in volume. Fold in the chocolate mixture.

In a separate bowl, and using a clean whisk attachment, beat the egg whites and cream of tartar at medium speed until soft peaks form. Gradually add the ¼ cup sugar, 1 tablespoon at a time, beating on high speed until stiff, glossy peaks form.

Fold one-third of the beaten whites into the chocolate mixture to lighten it. Then gently fold in the rest. Pour into the prepared ramekins and place on a baking sheet. Run the end of your thumb around the inside edge of the ramekins (this will help the soufflé rise evenly).

Bake on the middle rack for 15 minutes, or until puffed. The soufflé is done when it has puffed over the rim, the outside is golden, and the center jiggles slightly. Take care not to overbake. Serve immediately.

Flaky Apple Pie

Recipe courtesy of Sheetal Bhagat

The contestants were asked to create their own version of an American classic: apple pie. Sheetal's moutwatering recipe doesn't stray far from tradition and is stunning in its simplicity.

Graham Elliot says that this comforting, homey dessert is his favorite. After all, who doesn't love a slice of warm apple pie? Graham reflects, "When I think of family, I think of apple pie."

MAKES 1 PIE

3 pounds baking apples, such as
  Granny Smith and Pink Lady,
  peeled, cored, and thinly sliced

2 tablespoons all-purpose flour

Juice of ½ lemon

¾ cup light brown sugar, packed

¼ teaspoon ground cinnamon

¼ teaspoon freshly grated nutmeg

1 recipe Perfect Pie Crust (page 248)

2 tablespoons unsalted butter

1 large egg, lightly beaten with
  1 tablespoon water

1 tablespoon granulated sugar

Preheat the oven to 375°F.

In a medium bowl, combine the apples, flour, lemon juice, sugar, cinnamon, and nutmeg. Mix until the apples are well coated.

Remove the pie crust dough from the refrigerator. On a lightly floured surface, roll 1 disk of pastry into a circle to fit a 9- or 10-inch pie plate (see page 248).

To transfer the pastry to the pie plate, wrap it around a rolling pin and ease it into the pie plate. Be careful not to stretch the pastry. Trim it even with the edges of the pie plate.

Add the apple filling to the pastry-lined pie plate. Make sure the apple slices are lying flat. Cut the butter into small pieces and place on top of the filling.

Brush the top edges of the dough with the egg wash. Roll out the second disk of pie crust and place it over the top. Fold the top layer of dough under the edge of the bottom layer and press the edges together to form a seal. Flute the edges as desired.

Brush the surface of the dough with the egg wash and then sprinkle with the granulated sugar. Pierce the top of the dough in several places to allow steam to escape while baking.

Bake the pie on a baking sheet for 50 minutes, or until the crust is golden. Cover the edges with foil to prevent overbrowning if necessary. Cool on a rack before serving.

No-Bake Cheesecake with Graham Cracker Caramel Topping

Recipe courtesy of Whitney Miller

Whitney, the "pastry princess" from Mississippi, loves making cheesecake. While cheesecake can often take hours to bake, you don't even have to turn on the oven for this simple recipe because it doesn't contain any eggs. This creamy, rich, no-bake cheesecake stands on its head as well, with the crunchy, sweet graham cracker "crust" covering the top.

SERVES 4

8 graham crackers

6 tablespoons granulated sugar

2 tablespoons unsalted butter

1 pint fresh blackberries

2 (8-ounce) packages cream cheese, at room temperature

¾ cup confectioners' sugar, sifted

1 vanilla bean, split and scraped

2 tablespoons fresh lemon juice

⅔ cup heavy cream

Put the graham crackers in the food processor and pulse until finely ground. Put a small skillet over medium heat and add 4 tablespoons of the sugar. Cook until the sugar melts and begins to caramelize. Add the butter and stir to incorporate and melt. Add the graham cracker crumbles and toss. Pour the graham cracker caramel clusters onto a baking pan and set aside to cool.

Combine the remaining 2 tablespoons sugar with 2 tablespoons of water in a pot over medium heat. Cook for 1 to 2 minutes, or until the sugar is dissolved. Add the blackberries and toss. Cook for 3 to 5 minutes, or until the berries start to break down and form a sauce.

In a large bowl, beat the cream cheese on low speed for 1 minute, just until smooth and free of any lumps. Gradually add the confectioners' sugar and beat for 1 to 2 minutes, or until creamy. Periodically scrape down the sides of the bowl and the beaters. Add the vanilla bean seeds and lemon juice, beating until incorporated. The batter should be well mixed but not overbeaten.

In a separate, chilled bowl, whip the heavy cream for 2 minutes, or until soft peaks form. Gently fold the whipped cream into the cream cheese mixture.

Spoon the cream cheese mixture into 4 (3½-inch) ring molds on small serving plates. Level off the top with a butter knife. Chill for at least 40 minutes or up to overnight, until set.

Top with the graham cracker clusters and carefully remove the ring molds. Dress the plate with the blackberry compote.

Wedding Cookies

 Recipe courtesy of MasterChef **Kitchen**

These popular cookies got their name from being served at Mexican weddings as a sweet way to thank guests for sharing the day. In some parts of the country, they are made at Christmastime and are also known as butterballs or walnut balls. Regardless of the name, these delicious shortbread cookies with a pretty coating of powered sugar could not be easier to make and are perfect for any occasion. You can also substitute pecans or almonds for the walnuts, if you prefer.

MAKES 2 DOZEN (1¼-INCH) COOKIES

1 cup toasted walnuts

1 cup (2 sticks) unsalted butter,
   at room temperature

¼ cup granulated sugar

1 teaspoon pure vanilla extract

Pinch of salt

2 cups all-purpose flour

½ cup confectioners' sugar for
   rolling, plus more for dusting

Preheat the oven to 350°F.

Chop the nuts with a knife or pulse in a food processor until finely chopped but not powdery. Set aside.

Using a handheld or standing electric mixer, beat the butter on medium speed until very fluffy. Beat in the granulated sugar, vanilla, and salt until well blended. Gradually beat in the nuts and flour and continue to mix until fully incorporated.

Using your hands, roll the dough into balls the size of large marbles. Space them 1-inch apart on ungreased baking pans. Bake for 12 to 15 minutes, or until the cookies are lightly brown.

Remove from the oven. Put the confectioners' sugar in a small shallow bowl or pie plate. While still hot, roll the cookies in the sugar, a few at a time. Let cool on a plate or cooling rack. Dust with additional powdered sugar for a pretty presentation.

BASICS

Chicken Broth

 Recipe courtesy of MasterChef **Kitchen**

Making your own chicken broth is easy and adds incomparable flavor to any dish that calls for using stock. Homemade broth tastes better than canned or boxed broth and is a healthier option as it contains less sodium and no preservatives. Plus when you make chicken stock from scratch, your entire home will take on its warm, welcoming aroma.

MAKES 2 QUARTS

1 (3-pound) whole free-range chicken or leftover chicken parts, rinsed, giblets discarded

2 carrots, cut into large chunks

3 celery stalks, cut into large chunks

2 large white onions, quartered

1 garlic head, halved

¼ bunch fresh thyme

2 bay leaves

1 teaspoon whole black peppercorns

Put the chicken, carrots, celery, onions, and garlic in a large stockpot over medium heat. Pour in only enough cold water to cover (about 3 quarts). Too much will make the broth taste weak. Toss in the thyme, bay leaves, and peppercorns, and allow it to slowly come to a boil. Lower the heat to medium-low and gently simmer, uncovered, for 1 to 1½ hours, or until the chicken is done. As it cooks, skim any impurities that rise to the surface. Add a little more water, if necessary, to keep the chicken covered while simmering.

Carefully remove the chicken to a cutting board. When it's cool enough to handle, discard the skin and bones. Hand-shred the meat and place in a storage container to use as you wish.

Carefully strain the stock through a fine-mesh sieve into another pot to remove the vegetable solids. Use the broth immediately. If you plan on storing it, place the pot in a sink full of ice water and stir to cool down the broth. Cover and refrigerate for up to one week or freeze for up to two months.

Vegetable Broth

 Recipe courtesy of MasterChef **Kitchen**

The small amount of salt in this recipe helps draw out flavor from the vegetables as they simmer. Don't bother to peel the onion and garlic as the skins are loaded with flavor and vitamins.

MAKES 2 QUARTS

2 celery stalks, cut into large chunks

2 leeks, washed, trimmed, and halved (see Master the Basics: Cleaning Leeks, on page 83)

2 carrots, cut into large chunks

1 onion, halved

4 cloves garlic, smashed

1 teaspoon whole black peppercorns

6 sprigs fresh flat-leaf parsley

3 sprigs fresh thyme

2 bay leaves

1 teaspoon kosher salt

In a large stockpot, combine all of the ingredients with enough cold water to cover (about 1 gallon). Slowly bring to a boil over medium heat. Reduce the heat to low and gently simmer for 45 minutes, uncovered, skimming any impurities that rise to the surface. Turn off the heat and let the broth steep and settle for 10 minutes.

Strain the broth through a fine-mesh sieve into another pot to remove the solids. Use the broth immediately. If you plan on storing it, place the pot in a sink full of ice water and stir to cool down the broth. Cover and refrigerate for up to one week or freeze for up to two months.

Beef Broth

 Recipe courtesy of MasterChef Kitchen

Roasting soup bones in the oven first imparts a hearty beef flavor to this basic broth. In addition to using the broth in soups, use homemade beef broth to amp up flavor in stews, gravies, and sauces.

Though time-intensive, it's simple to make a rich demi-glace—a rich, flavorful sauce—by letting the broth slowly reduce.

MAKES 2 QUARTS

4 pounds meaty beef soup bones, such as short rib or shank

3 celery stalks, cut into large chunks

2 onions, quartered

1 carrot, cut into large chunks

1 garlic head, halved

1 teaspoon whole black peppercorns

2 bay leaves

3 sprigs fresh thyme

Preheat the oven to 425°F.

Arrange the beef bones in a large roasting pan in a single layer. Roast for 30 minutes, turning the bones once or twice, until they evenly brown on all sides. Add the celery, onions, carrot, and garlic. Roast for another 10 to 15 minutes, or until they brown on the edges.

Transfer the roasted bones and vegetables to a large stockpot. Put the roasting pan on two burners over medium-low flame. Pour in 1 cup of water and stir with a wooden spoon, scraping to release any caramelized bits that have stuck to the bottom of the pan. Pour this liquid into the stockpot, with enough additional water to cover the ingredients by 1 inch.

Add the peppercorns, bay leaves, and thyme to the pot. Bring the broth to a boil, reduce the heat to low, and gently simmer, uncovered, skimming any impurities that rise to the surface. Simmer for 3 hours, skimming occasionally and adding water as needed to keep the bones and vegetables covered at all times.

Strain the broth through a fine-mesh sieve into another pot to remove the solids. Remove any fat that may solidify on top. Use the broth immediately. If you plan on storing it, place the pot in a sink full of ice water and stir to cool down the broth. Cover and refrigerate for up to one week or freeze for up to two months.

To Make a Demi-Glace:

Slowly simmer the beef broth for 1 hour, until the liquid reduces down to a little more than 1 cup. The demi-glace should have deep color and be thick enough to coat the back of a spoon. If not using immediately, cover and refrigerate for up to one week or store in the freezer for up to one month.

Marinara Sauce

 Recipe courtesy of MasterChef Kitchen

The secret to a good marinara sauce lies in its simplicity. This straightforward marinara tastes pure, rich, round, and deeply reassuring, like a good tomato sauce is supposed to taste. This versatile sauce freezes well and lends itself to dozens of uses, making it a staple you should always have on hand in the freezer. The proportions can easily be doubled to create a larger batch.

It's important to use good-quality tomatoes. Joe Bastianich is a stickler for using the finest imported Italian plum tomatoes, such as his favorite, San Marzano. San Marzano is an heirloom variety of plum tomato, originally planted in the town of the same name at the base of Mount Vesuvius, near Naples. The volcanic soil and sunny climate grow tomatoes with a remarkable, sweet, intense flavor and mild acidity.

MAKES 2 QUARTS

½ cup extra-virgin olive oil

1 onion, finely chopped

4 cloves garlic, minced

2 bay leaves

Kosher salt and freshly ground
  black pepper

2 cans (28 ounces each) crushed
  tomatoes, preferably San
  Marzano

2 teaspoons dried oregano

6 fresh basil leaves, chopped

Coat a 3-quart pot with the oil and place over medium heat. When the oil is hot, add the onion, garlic, and bay leaves. Season with salt and pepper. Carefully add the tomatoes (with juice) and oregano. Cook, stirring occasionally, for 30 minutes, until the sauce is deep red and thick. Stir in the basil and season again with salt and pepper.

The sauce may be made a day ahead. Cool completely and store in a covered container in the refrigerator. Warm over medium heat before using. Oh, and whoever gets the bay leaves has to do the dishes!

Mayonnaise

 Recipe courtesy of MasterChef **Kitchen**

If you've been relying on the same old brands of jarred mayo for years, you'll be amazed at the bright, tangy flavor of homemade mayonnaise. Try making flavored mayo using herbs and spices, such as roasted garlic, saffron, or curry powder.

MAKES 2 CUPS

2 large egg yolks

2 teaspoons salt

2 teaspoons dry mustard

Dash of cayenne pepper

Juice of ½ lemon

2 cups canola oil

Have all of the ingredients at room temperature so that they will emulsify more readily. In a food processor or blender, combine the yolks, salt, mustard, cayenne, lemon juice, and 2 tablespoons of water. Process or blend to form a stable base.

With the motor running, add a few drops of the oil. The mixture will begin to thicken. Add the remaining oil in a thin, steady stream, scraping down the sides of the processor or blender. Check the seasoning. The mayo will keep covered in the refrigerator for up to 3 days.

Mustard Vinaigrette

 Recipe courtesy of MasterChef **Kitchen**

You'll never buy bottled dressing again after you taste this simple vinaigrette. Making dressing from scratch is infinitely more delicious, fresher, healthier, and super easy. This vinaigrette is a great starting point for interpretation and improvisation—create different flavors by substituting red wine, balsamic, or raspberry vinegar for the lemon. Or add fresh herbs such as chopped thyme or oregano.

MAKES ½ CUP

½ shallot, minced

1 teaspoon Dijon mustard

Juice of 1 lemon

¼ teaspoon kosher salt

⅛ teaspoon freshly ground
  black pepper

½ cup fruity extra-virgin olive oil

Combine the shallot, mustard, lemon juice, salt, and pepper in a bowl. Drizzle in the olive oil while whisking continuously.

Alternatively, combine all ingredients in a small jar with a tight-fitting lid. Shake vigorously for 30 seconds until emulsified.

Cooking Rice

 Recipe courtesy of MasterChef **Kitchen**

Say goodbye to sticky, undercooked, or overcooked rice! With the right technique, cooking rice perfectly is a snap. It's simple math—just remember: 1 cup dry rice + 2 cups water = 3 cups cooked rice.

MAKES 3 CUPS COOKED RICE

1 cup dry white rice

1 teaspoon salt

Combine the rice and 2 cups of water (double the amount of rice) in a pot. Sprinkle in the salt and bring to a boil over medium-high heat. When the liquid comes to a boil, reduce the heat to low and cover. Cook the rice for 15 minutes, without peeking under the lid—the steam is most precious to cooking rice. When the rice has absorbed the water, it will form "craters," or holes in the top.

Let the rice sit off the heat, undisturbed with the lid on, for at least 5 minutes. This allows the rice to steam, making the bottom layers as fluffy as the top.

Perfect Pie Crust

 Recipe courtesy of MasterChef Kitchen

The secret behind the great pie crust is using the right combination of both shortening and butter. The shortening lends the crust crumbliness, while the butter helps keep it flaky.

MAKES ONE 9- OR 10-INCH PIE CRUST

2 cups all-purpose flour, plus more for dusting

1 tablespoon sugar

1 teaspoon salt

½ cup (1 stick) very cold unsalted butter, cut into cubes

½ cup very cold vegetable shortening

Ice water (about 8 tablespoons)

In a large mixing bowl, combine the flour, sugar, and salt. Cut the butter and shortening into the flour by hand or with a pastry blender, until it's the texture of cornmeal. Sprinkle 1 tablespoon of ice water over the mixture and mix just until the dough is moistened.

Repeat by adding 6 to 8 tablespoons of ice water (one at a time) until all the dough is just moist. Take care not to overmix. Cut the dough in half and form each into a disk. Wrap the dough in plastic wrap and put in the refrigerator to chill while you make the filling.

Once the filling is ready, remove the dough from the refrigerator and follow the directions on the opposite page for rolling out a pie crust.

ROLLING OUT A PIE CRUST

1. Lightly flour your work surface. Place one disk of dough on the surface and roll it out using a rollng pin until the dough fits a 9- or 10-inch pie plate.

2. To transfer the dough to your pie plate, wrap it around the rolling pin and then unroll it onto the pie plate.

3. Press the dough into the sides of the plate, making sure the pastry fits into the corners snugly.

4. Trim the edges of the dough even with the edge of the pie plate.

5. Flute the edges in a decorative pattern, as desired.

For a double-crust pie, repeat the process and place the top crust atop the filled pie; seal the top and bottom layers by fluting the edges together.

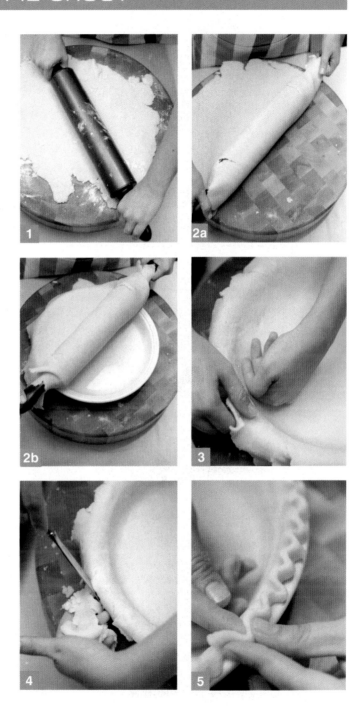

Acknowledgments

Loving what I do everyday is the absolute greatest joy in my life. Writing cookbooks and producing food television shows makes a hybrid career that characterizes my passion for cooking in a unique way. *MasterChef* has been one of the most gratifying and exciting experiences I've ever been involved in—I can't think of anyone who's got a better job.

I am extremely fortunate to work with the most creative, energetic, and talented people imaginable and would like to express my sincere gratitude.

Thank you to Liz Murdoch at Shine Group for your vision and leadership. You are the driving force of *MasterChef* and have created something of very special quality.

Massive thanks to the distinguished gentlemen at Reveille Productions—Mark Koops, H. T. Owens, Chad Bennett, and Robin Ashbrook—for cultivating this project and for always treating me like family.

We all owe our gratitude to Franc Rodham, the original UK format creator, as well as to Fox for their invaluable support of *MasterChef* in the United States.

To the top talent at 3-Ball Productions—J. D. Roth, Todd Nelson, Elayne Cilic, and Lisa Haese—thank you for being a dynamic creative force behind *MasterChef* and producing such a rewarding experience.

Thanks to Adeline Ramage Rooney at One Potato Two Potato for an endless stream of great ideas and supporting me through all the kitchen craziness.

Great appreciation to the indefatigable Lisa Shotland and her staff at CAA for taking good care of me and making it all happen.

To Julie Will, Pam Krauss, and everyone at Rodale: Thanks for the incredible effort and hard work it took to bring this project together.

Much love to Alesha Sin Vanata for your amazing food styling and for your unfailing good humor under pressure.

Props to Michele Chase for testing the recipes down to the last grain of salt and for possessing such an impeccable palate.

Thanks to Vanessa Stump for your vibrant photographs that effectively capture the delicious dishes of *MasterChef*.

To the best of the best: Gordon Ramsay, Joe Bastianich, and Graham Elliot. Thank you for sharing your knowledge, expertise, and passion. Your commitments to the craft of cooking are an inspiration to me.

Heartfelt gratitude to the *MasterChef* top 14 contestants, who are the heart and soul of this book. Thank you for trusting me to tell your story through food.

—JoAnn Cianciulli

Index

Underscored page references indicate sidebars. **Boldface** references indicate photographs.